To:

From:

The LORD bless you and keep you;

the LORD make his face shine upon you

and be gracious to you;

the LORD turn his face toward you and

give you peace.

Numbers 6:24-26

Promises for Students from the New International Version

ISBN 0-310-98263-4

Copyright 2000 by The Livingstone Corporation
All rights reserved

Requests for information should be addressed to:
    Inspirio, the Gift Group of Zondervan
    Grand Rapids, Michigan 49530

Developed and produced by The Livingstone Corporation

Project staff: Paige Haley, Christopher D. Hudson
Associate Editor: Molly C. Detweiler
Assistant Editor: Heidi Carvella
Design Manager and Interior design: Amy E. Langeler
Cover design: David Carlson

Printed in the United States

09 08 07 06 /OPM/ 15 14 13 12 11 10 9 8 7 6

Promises for Students

from the NIV

inspirio
The gift group of Zondervan

DEAR STUDENT,

AS YOU SET OUT ON THE NEW PATH BEFORE YOU, CLING TO THE PROMISES OF GOD. HE WILL BE FAITHFUL TO YOU AND WILL ENRICH YOUR LIFE WITH HIS GOOD AND PERFECT GIFTS. BECAUSE OF GOD, YOU HAVE GREAT CAUSE FOR CONFIDENCE.

"For I know the plans I have for you," declares the LORD, "plans to prosper you and not to harm you, plans to give you hope and a future. Then you will call upon me and come and pray to me, and I will listen to you. You will seek me and find me when you seek me with all your heart."

Jeremiah 29:11-13

Table of Contents

Chapter One

Can You Depend on God?

Promises about Who God Is

Thank you, God, for the rich
promises from your Word.
Your Word is true and offers
light for my path. Thank you
that I can depend on you at
all times and for every
need, because I can trust in
who you are. You never
change.

God Is Loving

Psalm 138:8
The LORD will fulfill his purpose for me;

your love, O LORD, endures forever—

do not abandon the works of your hands.

Jeremiah 31:3
The LORD appeared to us in the past, saying:

"I have loved you with an everlasting love;

I have drawn you with loving-kindness."

Psalm 145:8
The LORD is gracious and compassionate,

slow to anger and rich in love.

Lamentations 3:22–23
Because of the LORD's great love we are
not consumed,

for his compassions never fail.

They are new every morning;

great is your faithfulness.

Isaiah 40:11

The LORD tends his flock like a shepherd:

  He gathers the lambs in his arms

and carries them close to his heart;

  he gently leads those that have young.

Ephesians 2:4–5

Because of his great love for us, God, who is rich in
mercy, made us alive with Christ even when we
were dead in transgressions—it is by grace you
have been saved.

Isaiah 54:10

"Though the mountains be shaken

  and the hills be removed,

yet my unfailing love for you will not be shaken

  nor my covenant of peace be removed,"

  says the LORD, who has compassion on you.

1 Chronicles 16:34

Give thanks to the LORD, for he is good;

  his love endures forever.

Psalm 33:18

The eyes of the LORD are on those who fear him,

    on those whose hope is in his unfailing love.

Psalm 36:5, 7

Your love, O LORD, reaches to the heavens,

    your faithfulness to the skies. ...

    How priceless is your unfailing love!

Both high and low among men

    find refuge in the shadow of your wings.

Psalm 63:3

Because your love is better than life, O LORD,

    my lips will glorify you.

Psalm 103:11

As high as the heavens are above the earth,

    so great is God's love for those who fear him.

Ephesians 3:17–19

I pray that you, being rooted and established in love, may have power, together with all the saints, to grasp how wide and long and high and deep is the love of Christ, and to know this love that surpasses knowledge—that you may be filled to the measure of all the fullness of God.

1 John 3:16

This is how we know what love is: Jesus Christ laid down his life for us.

1 John 4:16

We know and rely on the love God has for us. God is love. Whoever lives in love lives in God, and God in him.

John 3:16

God so loved the world that he gave his one and only Son, that whoever believes in him shall not perish but have eternal life.

2 John 1:3

Grace, mercy and peace from God the Father and from Jesus Christ, the Father's Son, will be with us in truth and love.

Titus 3:4–5

When the kindness and love of God our Savior appeared, he saved us, not because of righteous things we had done, but because of his mercy.

Romans 8:38–39

I am convinced that neither death nor life, neither angels nor demons, neither the present nor the future, nor any powers, neither height nor depth, nor anything else in all creation, will be able to separate us from the love of God that is in Christ Jesus our Lord.

Romans 5:8

God demonstrates his own love for us in this: While we were still sinners, Christ died for us.

Romans 5:5
God has poured out his love into our hearts by the Holy Spirit, whom he has given us.

Zephaniah 3:17
The LORD your God is with you,

> he is mighty to save.

He will take great delight in you,

> he will quiet you with his love,

> he will rejoice over you with singing.

1 John 4:10–12
This is love: not that we loved God, but that he loved us and sent his Son as an atoning sacrifice for our sins. Dear friends, since God so loved us, we also ought to love one another. No one has ever seen God; but if we love one another, God lives in us and his love is made complete in us.

1 John 4:18
There is no fear in love. But perfect love drives out fear.

1 John 3:1
How great is the love the Father has lavished on us, that we should be called children of God! And that is what we are!

2 Thessalonians 2:16–17
May our Lord Jesus Christ himself and God our Father, who loved us and by his grace gave us eternal encouragement and good hope, encourage your hearts and strengthen you in every good deed and word.

Ephesians 5:2
Live a life of love, just as Christ loved us and gave himself up for us as a fragrant offering and sacrifice to God.

Ephesians 1:4–6

In love God predestined us to be adopted as his sons through Jesus Christ, in accordance with his pleasure and will—to the praise of his glorious grace, which he has freely given us in the One he loves.

2 Corinthians 13:14

May the grace of the Lord Jesus Christ, and the love of God, and the fellowship of the Holy Spirit be with you.

My favorite verses about the love of God

_____

_____

_____

_____

_____

_____

_____

_____

_____

_____

_____

_____

_____

_____

_____

_____

_____

Thoughts and Reflections about the love of God

_____

_____

_____

_____

_____

_____

_____

_____

_____

_____

_____

_____

_____

_____

_____

_____

_____

_____

God Is Gracious

Psalm 86:15

You, O Lord, are a compassionate
and gracious God,

slow to anger, abounding in love
and faithfulness.

James 5:11

The Lord is full of compassion and mercy.

Isaiah 30:18

The LORD longs to be gracious to you;

he rises to show you compassion.

For the LORD is a God of justice.

Blessed are all who wait for him!

Isaiah 33:2

O LORD, be gracious to us;

we long for you.

Be our strength every morning,

our salvation in time of distress.

Isaiah 38:17

In your love you kept me

from the pit of destruction, O LORD;

you have put all my sins

behind your back.

Titus 3:5–6

God saved us, not because of righteous things we
had done, but because of his mercy. He saved us
through the washing of rebirth and renewal by the
Holy Spirit, whom he poured out on us generously
through Jesus Christ our Savior.

1 Peter 1:3

Praise be to the God and Father of our Lord Jesus
Christ! In his great mercy he has given us new
birth into a living hope through the resurrection of
Jesus Christ from the dead.

Psalm 51:1

Have mercy on me, O God,

according to your unfailing love;

according to your great compassion

blot out my transgressions.

Psalm 116:1

I love the LORD, for he heard my voice;

he heard my cry for mercy.

Micah 7:18

Who is a God like you,

who pardons sin

and forgives the transgression

of the remnant of his inheritance?

You do not stay angry forever

but delight to show mercy.

2 Corinthians 12:9

The Lord said to me, "My grace is sufficient for
you, for my power is made perfect in weakness."
Therefore I will boast all the more gladly about my
weaknesses, so that Christ's power may rest on me.

2 Peter 3:18
Grow in the grace and knowledge of our Lord and Savior Jesus Christ. To him be glory both now and forever! Amen.

2 Chronicles 30:9
The LORD your God is gracious and compassionate. He will not turn his face from you if you return to him.

Ephesians 1:7–8
In Christ we have redemption through his blood, the forgiveness of sins, in accordance with the riches of God's grace that he lavished on us with all wisdom and understanding.

My favorite verses about the graciousness of God

_____
_____
_____
_____
_____
_____
_____
_____
_____
_____
_____
_____
_____
_____
_____

Thoughts and Reflections about the graciousness of God

_____

_____

_____

_____

_____

_____

_____

_____

_____

_____

_____

_____

_____

_____

_____

_____

God Is Strong

Psalm 46:1
God is our refuge and strength,

an ever-present help in trouble.

Psalm 73:26
My flesh and my heart may fail,

but God is the strength of my heart

and my portion forever.

Proverbs 18:10
The name of the LORD is a strong tower;

the righteous run to it and are safe.

Psalm 28:7
The LORD is my strength and my shield;

my heart trusts in him, and I am helped.

Psalm 18:1
I love you, O LORD, my strength.

Psalm 84:5
Blessed are those whose strength is in you, O LORD.

Habakkuk 3:19
The Sovereign LORD is my strength;

> he makes my feet like the feet of a deer,

> he enables me to go on the heights.

Ephesians 6:10
Be strong in the Lord and in his mighty power.

Psalm 59:9
O my Strength, I watch for you;

> you, O God, are my fortress, my loving God.

Isaiah 33:2
O LORD, be gracious to us;

> we long for you.

Be our strength every morning,

> our salvation in time of distress.

Psalm 27:1

The LORD is my light and my salvation—

> whom shall I fear?

The LORD is the stronghold of my life—

> of whom shall I be afraid?

2 Samuel 22:33

It is God who arms me with

> strength and makes my way perfect.

Psalm 16:5, 8

LORD, you have assigned me my portion and my cup;

> you have made my lot secure. ...

I have set the LORD always before me.

> Because he is at my right hand,

> I will not be shaken.

Psalm 55:22

Cast your cares on the LORD

> and he will sustain you;

> he will never let the righteous fall.

Psalm 59:16

I will sing of your strength, O LORD,

in the morning I will sing of your love;

for you are my fortress,

my refuge in times of trouble.

Hebrews 13:6

We say with confidence, "The LORD is my helper; I will not be afraid. What can man do to me?"

Deuteronomy 33:27

The eternal God is your refuge,

and underneath are the everlasting arms.

2 Samuel 22:31

As for God, his way is perfect;

the word of the LORD is flawless.

He is a shield

for all who take refuge in him.

Psalm 4:8

I will lie down and sleep in peace,

for you alone, O LORD,

make me dwell in safety.

Psalm 17:7–8

Show the wonder of your great love, O LORD,

you who save by your right hand

those who take refuge in you from their foes.

Keep me as the apple of your eye;

hide me in the shadow of your wings.

Psalm 32:7

You are my hiding place, O God;

you will protect me from trouble

and surround me with songs of deliverance.

Psalm 46:5–7

God is within [Jerusalem], she will not fall;

God will help her at break of day.

Nations are in uproar, kingdoms fall;

he lifts his voice, the earth melts.

The LORD Almighty is with us;

the God of Jacob is our fortress.

Psalm 91:14–15

"Because he loves me," says the LORD,

"I will rescue him;

I will protect him,

for he acknowledges my name.

He will call upon me, and I will answer him;

I will be with him in trouble,

I will deliver him and honor him."

Psalm 116:6

The LORD protects the simplehearted;

when I was in great need, he saved me.

Isaiah 41:10

"Do not fear, for I am with you;

>   do not be dismayed, for I am your God.

I will strengthen you and help you;

>   I will uphold you with
>>   my righteous right hand."

Isaiah 43:1–2

"Fear not, for I have redeemed you;

>   I have summoned you by name; you are mine.

When you pass through the waters,

>   I will be with you;

and when you pass through the rivers,

>   they will not sweep over you.

When you walk through the fire,

>   you will not be burned;

the flames will not set you ablaze."

>>>   says the LORD.

Nahum 1:7
The LORD is good,

> a refuge in times of trouble.

He cares for those who trust in him.

2 Thessalonians 3:3
The Lord is faithful, and he will strengthen and protect you from the evil one.

Nehemiah 8:10
The joy of the LORD is your strength.

Philippians 4:13
I can do everything through God who gives me strength.

My favorite verses about the strength of God

_____

_____

_____

_____

_____

_____

_____

_____

_____

_____

_____

_____

_____

_____

_____

_____

_____

_____

Thoughts and Reflections about the strength of God

_____

_____

_____

_____

_____

_____

_____

_____

_____

_____

_____

_____

_____

_____

_____

_____

God Is Faithful

1 John 1:9
If we confess our sins, God is faithful and just and
will forgive us our sins and purify us from all
unrighteousness.

Deuteronomy 7:9
Know therefore that the LORD your God is God; he
is the faithful God, keeping his covenant of love to
a thousand generations of those who love him and
keep his commands.

Psalm 91:1–2, 4
He who dwells in the shelter of the Most High
　　will rest in the shadow of the Almighty.
I will say of the LORD, "He is my refuge and my
　　　fortress,
　　my God, in whom I trust." ...
He will cover you with his feathers,
　　and under his wings you will find refuge;
　　his faithfulness will be your shield and rampart.

Psalm 100:5

The LORD is good and his love endures forever;

> his faithfulness continues
>> through all generations.

Psalm 108:4

Great is your love, O LORD, higher than the heavens;

> your faithfulness reaches to the skies.

Psalm 121:3–8

The LORD will not let your foot slip—

> he who watches over you will not slumber;

indeed, he who watches over Israel

> will neither slumber nor sleep.

The LORD watches over you—

> the LORD is your shade at your right hand;

the sun will not harm you by day,

> nor the moon by night.

The LORD will keep you from all harm—

> he will watch over your life;

the LORD will watch over your coming and going

> both now and forevermore.

Lamentations 3:22–23
Because of the LORD's great love we are not consumed,

for his compassions never fail.

They are new every morning;

great is your faithfulness.

1 Corinthians 1:9
God, who has called you into fellowship with his
Son Jesus Christ our Lord, is faithful.

2 Thessalonians 3:3
The Lord is faithful, and he will strengthen and
protect you from the evil one.

Deuteronomy 32:4
God is the Rock, his works are perfect,

and all his ways are just.

A faithful God who does no wrong,

upright and just is he.

Psalm 33:4

The word of the LORD is right and true;

> he is faithful in all he does.

Psalm 86:15

You, O LORD, are a compassionate and gracious
God,

> slow to anger, abounding in love
> and faithfulness.

Psalm 115:1

Not to us, O LORD, not to us

> but to your name be the glory,

> because of your love and faithfulness.

Psalm 138:8

The LORD will fulfill his purpose for me;

> your love, O LORD, endures forever—

> do not abandon the works of your hands.

1 Corinthians 10:13
God is faithful; he will not let you be tempted beyond what you can bear. But when you are tempted, he will also provide a way out so that you can stand up under it.

1 Thessalonians 5:23–24
May God himself, the God of peace, sanctify you through and through. May your whole spirit, soul and body be kept blameless at the coming of our Lord Jesus Christ. The one who calls you is faithful and he will do it.

2 Timothy 2:13
If we are faithless,

Christ will remain faithful.

Hebrews 10:23
Let us hold unswervingly to the hope we profess, for God who promised is faithful.

Psalm 23:1
The LORD is my shepherd, I shall not be in want.

Acts 14:17
God has not left himself without testimony: He has shown kindness by giving you rain from heaven and crops in their seasons; he provides you with plenty of food and fills your hearts with joy.

2 Corinthians 9:8
God is able to make all grace abound to you, so that in all things at all times, having all that you need, you will abound in every good work.

Philippians 4:19
God will meet all your needs according to his glorious riches in Christ Jesus.

My favorite verses about the faithfulness of God

_____

_____

_____

_____

_____

_____

_____

_____

_____

_____

_____

_____

_____

_____

_____

_____

_____

_____

Thoughts and Reflections about the faithfulness of God

_____

_____

_____

_____

_____

_____

_____

_____

_____

_____

_____

_____

_____

_____

_____

_____

God Is Compassionate

Psalm 145:8
The LORD is gracious and compassionate,

slow to anger and rich in love.

Isaiah 30:18
The LORD longs to be gracious to you;

he rises to show you compassion.

For the LORD is a God of justice.

Blessed are all who wait for him!

Psalm 119:156
Your compassion is great, O LORD;

preserve my life according to your laws.

Isaiah 54:10
"Though the mountains be shaken

and the hills be removed,

yet my unfailing love for you will not be shaken

nor my covenant of peace be removed,"

says the LORD, who has compassion on you.

Psalm 145:9

The LORD is good to all;

he has compassion on all he has made.

Hosea 2:19

"I will betroth you to me forever;

I will betroth you in righteousness and justice,

in love and compassion,"

declares the LORD.

Exodus 33:19

The LORD said, "I will cause all my goodness to pass in front of you, and I will proclaim my name, the LORD, in your presence. I will have mercy on whom I will have mercy, and I will have compassion on whom I will have compassion."

Psalm 103:2–5

Praise the LORD, O my soul,

and forget not all his benefits—

who forgives all your sins

and heals all your diseases,

who redeems your life from the pit

and crowns you with love and compassion,

who satisfies your desires with good things

so that your youth is renewed like the eagle's.

Psalm 111:4

God has caused his wonders to be remembered;

the LORD is gracious and compassionate.

Isaiah 49:10, 13

They will neither hunger nor thirst,

> nor will the desert heat or the sun beat upon
> them.

God who has compassion on them will guide them

> and lead them beside springs of water. ...

Shout for joy, O heavens;

> rejoice, O earth;

> burst into song, O mountains!

For the LORD comforts his people

> and will have compassion on his afflicted ones.

2 Corinthians 1:3

Praise be to the God and Father of our Lord Jesus
Christ, the Father of compassion and the God of
all comfort.

Ephesians 4:32

Be kind and compassionate to one another, forgiving each other, just as in Christ God forgave you.

Psalm 103:11–13

As high as the heavens are above the earth,

  so great is God's love for those who fear him;

as far as the east is from the west,

  so far has he removed our transgressions from us.

As a father has compassion on his children,

  so the LORD has compassion on those who fear
him.

James 5:11

The Lord is full of compassion and mercy.

Lamentations 3:32

God will show compassion,

  so great is his unfailing love.

Isaiah 54:8

"With everlasting kindness

  I will have compassion on you,"

  says the LORD your Redeemer.

Micah 7:18–19
Who is a God like you,

who pardons sin and forgives the
transgression
of the remnant of his
inheritance?

You do not stay angry forever

but delight to show mercy.

You will again have compassion on us;

you will tread our sins underfoot

and hurl all our iniquities into the depths of
the sea.

My favorite verses about the compassion of God

_____
_____
_____
_____
_____
_____
_____
_____
_____
_____
_____
_____
_____
_____
_____
_____
_____
_____

Thoughts and Reflections about the compassion of God

_____

_____

_____

_____

_____

_____

_____

_____

_____

_____

_____

_____

_____

_____

_____

_____

_____

Chapter Two

Who Is God to You?

*Promises about God's Role in
Your Life*

Thank you, my Lord, that you are a personal God. You made me in your own image and designed me to have a relationship with you. Thank you that you are all things to me and you meet my every need. Every time I seek you, you reveal your-self to me in new and refreshing ways.

God Is your Savior

John 3:16
God so loved the world that he gave his one and
only Son, that whoever believes in him shall not
perish but have eternal life.

Romans 5:8
God demonstrates his own love for us in this:
While we were still sinners, Christ died for us.

1 John 4:10
This is love: not that we loved God, but that he
loved us and sent his Son as an atoning sacrifice
for our sins.

Isaiah 53:5
He was pierced for our transgressions,

he was crushed for our iniquities;
the punishment that brought us peace was upon
him,

and by his wounds we are healed.

1 Peter 1:18–19

You know that it was not with perishable things such as silver or gold that you were redeemed ... but with the precious blood of Christ, a lamb without blemish or defect.

1 John 2:2

Jesus Christ is the atoning sacrifice for our sins, and not only for ours but also for the sins of the whole world.

Isaiah 1:18

"Come now, let us reason together,"

    says the LORD.

"Though your sins are like scarlet,

    they shall be as white as snow;

though they are red as crimson,

    they shall be like wool."

Isaiah 43:25

"I, even I, am he who blots out

　　your transgressions, for my own sake,

　　and remembers your sins no more,"

　　　declares the LORD.

Acts 2:38

Peter said, "Repent and be baptized, every one of
you, in the name of Jesus Christ for the forgiveness of your sins. And you will receive the gift of
the Holy Spirit."

Ephesians 1:7

In Christ we have redemption through his blood,
the forgiveness of sins, in accordance with the
riches of God's grace.

John 3:36

Whoever believes in the Son has eternal life.

Colossians 2:13-14
When you were dead in your sins and in the uncir-
cumcision of your sinful nature, God made you
alive with Christ. He forgave us all our sins, having
canceled the written code, with its regulations,
that was against us and that stood opposed to us;
he took it away, nailing it to the cross.

1 John 1:9
If we confess our sins, God is faithful and just and
will forgive us our sins and purify us from all
unrighteousness.

Romans 10:10
It is with your heart that you believe and are justified, and it is with your mouth that you confess
and are saved.

Ezekiel 36:26
God said, "I will give you a new heart and put a
new spirit in you; I will remove from you your
heart of stone and give you a heart of flesh."

2 Corinthians 5:17
If anyone is in Christ, he is a new creation; the old
has gone, the new has come!

Ephesians 2:4–5
Because of his great love for us, God, who is rich in
mercy, made us alive with Christ even when we
were dead in transgressions—it is by grace you
have been saved.

Psalm 62:1–2
My soul finds rest in God alone;

> my salvation comes from him.

He alone is my rock and my salvation;

> he is my fortress, I will never be shaken.

Isaiah 44:22
"I have swept away your offenses like a cloud,

> your sins like the morning mist.

Return to me,

> for I have redeemed you,"

>> declares the LORD.

Lamentations 3:57–58

You came near when I called you,

and you said, "Do not fear."

O LORD, you took up my case;

you redeemed my life.

Acts 10:43

All the prophets testify about Jesus that everyone who believes in him receives forgiveness of sins through his name.

Romans 10:9

If you confess with your mouth, "Jesus is Lord," and believe in your heart that God raised him from the dead, you will be saved.

2 Corinthians 6:2

God says, "In the time of my favor I heard you, and in the day of salvation I helped you."

I tell you, now is the time of God's favor, now is the day of salvation.

Ephesians 2:13
Now in Christ Jesus you who once were far away
have been brought near through the blood of
Christ.

Colossians 1:13–14
God has rescued us from the dominion of darkness
and brought us into the kingdom of the Son he
loves, in whom we have redemption, the forgiveness of sins.

Titus 3:5
God saved us, not because of righteous things we
had done, but because of his mercy. He saved us
through the washing of rebirth and renewal by the
Holy Spirit.

1 Peter 2:24
Christ himself bore our sins in his body on the tree,
so that we might die to sins and live for righteousness; by his wounds you have been healed.

John 14:6
Jesus said, "I am the way and the truth and the life. No one comes to the Father except through me."

1 John 5:18
We know that anyone born of God does not continue to sin; the one who was born of God keeps him safe, and the evil one cannot harm him.

1 Peter 1:3–5
Praise be to the God and Father of our Lord Jesus Christ! In his great mercy he has given us new birth into a living hope through the resurrection of Jesus Christ from the dead, and into an inheritance that can never perish, spoil or fade—kept in heaven for you, who through faith are shielded by God's power until the coming of the salvation that is ready to be revealed in the last time.

My favorite verses about God as my Savior

_____

_____

_____

_____

_____

_____

_____

_____

_____

_____

_____

_____

_____

_____

_____

_____

Thoughts and Reflections about God as my Savior

_____

_____

_____

_____

_____

_____

_____

_____

_____

_____

_____

_____

_____

_____

_____

God Is Your Shepherd

Psalm 23:1
The LORD is my shepherd, I shall not be in want.

John 10:14–16
Jesus said, "I am the good shepherd; I know my sheep and my sheep know me—just as the Father knows me and I know the Father—and I lay down my life for the sheep. I have other sheep that are not of this sheep pen. I must bring them also. They too will listen to my voice, and there shall be one flock and one shepherd."

Psalm 28:9
Save your people and bless
   your inheritance, O LORD;

   be their shepherd and carry them forever.

Psalm 78:52
God brought his people out like a flock;

   he led them like sheep through the desert.

Psalm 95:7
He is our God

> and we are the people of his pasture,
>
> the flock under his care.

Psalm 100:3
Know that the LORD is God.

> It is he who made us, and we are his.

Isaiah 40:11
The LORD tends his flock like a shepherd:

> He gathers the lambs in his arms
and carries them close to his heart;

> he gently leads those that have young.

Jeremiah 23:3
"I myself will gather the remnant of my flock out
of all the countries where I have driven them and
will bring them back to their pasture, where they
will be fruitful and increase in number," declares
the LORD.

Jeremiah 31:10

Hear the word of the LORD, O nations;

    proclaim it in distant coastlands:

"He who scattered Israel will gather them

    and will watch over his flock like a shepherd."

Ezekiel 34:11–12

This is what the Sovereign LORD says: "I myself will search for my sheep and look after them. As a shepherd looks after his scattered flock when he is with them, so will I look after my sheep. I will rescue them from all the places where they were scattered on a day of clouds and darkness."

Ezekiel 34:15–16

"I myself will tend my sheep and have them lie down," declares the Sovereign LORD. "I will search for the lost and bring back the strays. I will bind up the injured and strengthen the weak."

Ezekiel 34:31

"You my sheep, the sheep of my pasture, are people, and I am your God," declares the Sovereign LORD.

Zechariah 9:16

The Lord their God will save them on that day
    as the flock of his people.
They will sparkle in his land
    like jewels in a crown.

Mark 6:34

When Jesus ... saw a large crowd, he had compassion on them, because they were like sheep without a shepherd. So he began teaching them many things.

Luke 12:32

Do not be afraid, little flock, for your Father has been pleased to give you the kingdom.

1 Peter 2:25
You were like sheep going astray, but now you have returned to the Shepherd and Overseer of your souls.

Revelation 7:17
The Lamb at the center of the throne will be their shepherd; he will lead them to springs of living water. And God will wipe away every tear from their eyes.

Hebrews 13:20–21
May the God of peace, who through the blood of the eternal covenant brought back from the dead our Lord Jesus, that great Shepherd of the sheep, equip you with everything good for doing his will, and may he work in us what is pleasing to him, through Jesus Christ, to whom be glory for ever and ever.

John 10:27–30
Jesus said, "My sheep listen to my voice; I know
them, and they follow me. I give them eternal life,
and they shall never perish; no one can snatch
them out of my hand. My Father, who has given
them to me, is greater than all; no one can snatch
them out of my Father's hand. I and the Father are
one."

My favorite verses about God as my shepherd

_____

_____

_____

_____

_____

_____

_____

_____

_____

_____

_____

_____

_____

_____

_____

_____

_____

_____

Thoughts and Reflections about God as my shepherd

_____

_____

_____

_____

_____

_____

_____

_____

_____

_____

_____

_____

_____

_____

_____

_____

_____

God Is Your Friend

John 15:15

Jesus said, "I no longer call you servants, because a servant does not know his master's business. Instead, I have called you friends, for everything that I learned from my Father I have made known to you."

Hosea 11:4

"I led them with cords of human kindness,

with ties of love;

I lifted the yoke from their neck

and bent down to feed them, "

declares the LORD.

John 14:23

Jesus said, "If anyone loves me, he will obey my teaching. My Father will love him, and we will come to him and make our home with him."

Jeremiah 15:15
You understand, O LORD;

remember me and care for me.

James 2:23
The scripture was fulfilled that says, "Abraham
believed God, and it was credited to him as righteousness," and he was called God's friend.

Revelation 3:20
Jesus said, "Here I am! I stand at the door and
knock. If anyone hears my voice and opens the
door, I will come in and eat with him, and he with
me."

1 Corinthians 1:9
God, who has called you into fellowship with his
Son Jesus Christ our Lord, is faithful.

1 Peter 5:7
Cast all your anxiety on God because he cares for
you.

1 John 1:3
Our fellowship is with the Father and with his Son,
Jesus Christ.

Deuteronomy 30:20
Love the LORD your God, listen to his voice, and
hold fast to him. For the LORD is your life.

John 14:21
Jesus said, "He who loves me will be loved by my
Father, and I too will love him and show myself to
him."

Psalm 27:10
Though my father and mother forsake me,

    the LORD will receive me.

John 14:18
Jesus said, "I will not leave you as orphans; I will
come to you."

John 15:12–14

Jesus said, "Love each other as I have loved you. Greater love has no one than this, that he lay down his life for his friends. You are my friends if you do what I command."

Proverbs 18:24

There is a friend who sticks closer than a brother.

Isaiah 43:4

"You are precious and honored in my sight, and ... I love you," says the LORD.

My favorite verses about God as my friend

_____

_____

_____

_____

_____

_____

_____

_____

_____

_____

_____

_____

_____

_____

_____

_____

_____

_____

Thoughts and Reflections about God as my friend

_____

_____

_____

_____

_____

_____

_____

_____

_____

_____

_____

_____

_____

_____

God Is Your Lord

Philippians 2:9–11
God exalted Christ to the highest place
and gave him the name
that is above every name,
that at the name of Jesus every knee should bow,
in heaven and on earth and under the earth,
and every tongue confess that Jesus Christ is Lord,
to the glory of God the Father.

Romans 10:9
If you confess with your mouth, "Jesus is Lord,"
and believe in your heart that God raised him from
the dead, you will be saved.

Isaiah 50:7
Because the Sovereign LORD helps me,
I will not be disgraced.
Therefore have I set my face like flint,
and I know I will not be put to shame.

Acts 2:25
David said about God:
"I saw the Lord always before me.

> Because he is at my right hand,

> I will not be shaken."

Acts 2:36
Let all Israel be assured of this: God has made this
Jesus, ... both Lord and Christ.

Romans 14:8
If we live, we live to the Lord; and if we die, we die
to the Lord. So, whether we live or die, we belong
to the Lord.

Psalm 16:2
I said to the LORD, "You are my LORD;

> apart from you I have no good thing."

Psalm 89:8
O LORD God Almighty, who is like you?

> You are mighty, O LORD, and your faithfulness
surrounds you.

Jeremiah 15:16

When your words came, I ate them;

they were my joy and my heart's delight,

for I bear your name,

O LORD God Almighty.

Hosea 12:5

The LORD God Almighty,

the LORD is his name of renown!

Amos 4:13

He who forms the mountains,

creates the wind,

and reveals his thoughts to man,

he who turns dawn to darkness,

and treads the high places of the earth—

the LORD God Almighty is his name.

Revelation 4:8

Holy, holy, holy

is the Lord God Almighty,

who was, and is, and is to come.

Revelation 11:17

We give thanks to you, Lord God Almighty,

the One who is and who was,

because you have taken your great power

and have begun to reign.

Revelation 15:3

Great and marvelous are your deeds,

Lord God Almighty.

Just and true are your ways,

King of the ages.

Romans 6:22

Now that you have been set free from sin and
have become slaves to God, the benefit you reap
leads to holiness, and the result is eternal life.

Psalm 84:11

The LORD God is a sun and shield;

the LORD bestows favor and honor;

no good thing does he withhold

from those whose walk is blameless.

Psalm 11:7

The LORD is righteous,

he loves justice;

upright men will see his face.

Psalm 103:6

The LORD works righteousness

and justice for all the oppressed.

Acts 17:27

God is not far from each one of us.

Psalm 139:9–10

If I rise on the wings of the dawn,

if I settle on the far side of the sea,

even there your hand will guide me, O LORD,

your right hand will hold me fast.

Isaiah 43:2-3

"When you pass through the waters,

I will be with you;

and when you pass through the rivers,

they will not sweep over you.

When you walk through the fire,

you will not be burned;

the flames will not set you ablaze.

For I am the LORD, your God,

the Holy One of Israel, your Savior."

Psalm 145:18
The LORD is near to all who call on him,

 to all who call on him in truth.

Deuteronomy 31:6
Be strong and courageous. Do not be afraid or terrified ... for the LORD your God goes with you; he will never leave you nor forsake you.

Deuteronomy 4:7
What other nation is so great as to have their gods near them the way the LORD our God is near us whenever we pray to him?

Psalm 145:17
The LORD is righteous in all his ways

 and loving toward all he has made.

Psalm 119:137
Righteous are you, O LORD,

> and your laws are right.

Revelation 11:15
The kingdom of the world has become the kingdom of our Lord and of his Christ, and he will
reign for ever and ever.

Romans 4:20–25
Abraham did not waver through unbelief regard-
ing the promise of God, but was strengthened in
his faith and gave glory to God, being fully per-
suaded that God had power to do what he had
promised. This is why "it was credited to him as
righteousness." The words "it was credited to him"
were written not for him alone, but also for us, to
whom God will credit righteousness—for us who
believe in him who raised Jesus our Lord from the
dead. He was delivered over to death for our sins
and was raised to life for our justification.

My favorite verses about God as my Lord

_____

_____

_____

_____

_____

_____

_____

_____

_____

_____

_____

_____

_____

_____

_____

Thoughts and Reflections about God as my Lord

_____

_____

_____

_____

_____

_____

_____

_____

_____

_____

_____

_____

_____

_____

_____

God Is Your Father

Isaiah 64:8
O LORD, you are our Father.

> We are the clay, you are the potter;
>
> we are all the work of your hand.

2 Corinthians 6:18
"I will be a Father to you,

> and you will be my sons and daughters,"
>
> says the Lord Almighty.

Matthew 5:16
Let your light shine before men, that they may see your good deeds and praise your Father in heaven.

Matthew 6:6
When you pray, go into your room, close the door and pray to your Father, who is unseen. Then your Father, who sees what is done in secret, will reward you.

Matthew 6:14
If you forgive men when they sin against you, your heavenly Father will also forgive you.

Matthew 6:26
Look at the birds of the air; they do not sow or reap or store away in barns, and yet your heavenly Father feeds them. Are you not much more valuable than they?

Matthew 18:19
Jesus said, "If two of you on earth agree about anything you ask for, it will be done for you by my Father in heaven."

Matthew 7:11
If you ... know how to give good gifts to your children, how much more will your Father in heaven give good gifts to those who ask him!

Matthew 10:29, 31
Are not two sparrows sold for a penny? Yet not one of them will fall to the ground apart from the will of your Father. ... So don't be afraid; you are worth more than many sparrows.

John 6:57
Jesus said, "Just as the living Father sent me and I live because of the Father, so the one who feeds on me will live because of me."

Isaiah 9:6
To us a child is born,

    to us a son is given,

    and the government will be on his shoulders.

And he will be called

    Wonderful Counselor, Mighty God,

    Everlasting Father, Prince of Peace.

Luke 12:32
Do not be afraid, little flock, for your Father has been pleased to give you the kingdom.

1 Corinthians 8:6
For us there is but one God, the Father, from whom all things came and for whom we live; and there is but one Lord, Jesus Christ, through whom all things came and through whom we live.

2 Corinthians 1:3
Praise be to the God and Father of our Lord Jesus Christ, the Father of compassion and the God of all comfort.

Hebrews 12:9
We have all had human fathers who disciplined us and we respected them for it. How much more should we submit to the Father of our spirits and live!

John 15:9
Jesus said, "As the Father has loved me, so have I loved you."

John 14:6
Jesus said, "I am the way and the truth and the life. No one comes to the Father except through me."

James 1:17
Every good and perfect gift is from above, coming down from the Father of the heavenly lights, who does not change like shifting shadows.

1 John 2:23
Whoever acknowledges the Son has the Father also.

1 John 3:1
How great is the love the Father has lavished on us, that we should be called children of God! And that is what we are!

John 1:12–13

To all who received Christ, to those who believed in his name, he gave the right to become children of God—children born not of natural descent, nor of human decision or a husband's will, but born of God.

Romans 8:14–16

Those who are led by the Spirit of God are sons of God. For you did not receive a spirit that makes you a slave again to fear, but you received the Spirit of sonship. And by him we cry, "*Abba,* Father." The Spirit himself testifies with our spirit that we are God's children.

1 John 3:2

Dear friends, now we are children of God, and what we will be has not yet been made known. But we know that when he appears, we shall be like him, for we shall see him as he is.

Galatians 4:6–7

Because you are sons, God sent the Spirit of his Son into our hearts, the Spirit who calls out, "*Abba*, Father." So you are no longer a slave, but a son; and since you are a son, God has made you also an heir.

Ephesians 5:1–2

Be imitators of God, therefore, as dearly loved children and live a life of love, just as Christ loved us and gave himself up for us as a fragrant offering and sacrifice to God.

1 John 5:2–4

This is how we know that we love the children of God: by loving God and carrying out his commands. This is love for God: to obey his commands. And his commands are not burdensome, for everyone born of God overcomes the world. This is the victory that has overcome the world, even our faith.

Galatians 3:26, 28
You are all sons of God through faith in Christ Jesus.
... There is neither Jew nor Greek, slave nor free,
male nor female, for you are all one in Christ Jesus.

1 John 4:14–15
We have seen and testify that the Father has sent
his Son to be the Savior of the world. If anyone
acknowledges that Jesus is the Son of God, God
lives in him and he in God.

My favorite verses about God as my Father

_____

_____

_____

_____

_____

_____

_____

_____

_____

_____

_____

_____

_____

_____

_____

_____

_____

Thoughts and Reflections about God as my Father

_____

_____

_____

_____

_____

_____

_____

_____

_____

_____

_____

_____

_____

_____

_____

_____

Chapter Three

Does God Hold Your Future?
Promises about God's Guidance

Thank you, God, that you have engraved me on the palm of your hand. You hold my future, so I never have reason to fear. Through you I have the gift of eternal life, and your faithful guidance makes my life full.

Eternal Life

John 3:16
God so loved the world that he gave his one and only Son, that whoever believes in him shall not perish but have eternal life.

1 John 2:17
The world and its desires pass away, but the man who does the will of God lives forever.

Romans 6:23
The gift of God is eternal life in Christ Jesus our Lord.

John 3:36
Whoever believes in the Son has eternal life.

John 17:3
This is eternal life: that they may know you, the only true God, and Jesus Christ, whom you have sent.

Hebrews 5:9
Once made perfect, Jesus became the source of
eternal salvation for all who obey him.

Psalm 62:1–2
My soul finds rest in God alone;

 my salvation comes from him.
He alone is my rock and my salvation;

 he is my fortress, I will never be shaken.

1 John 5:11–12
God has given us eternal life, and this life is in his
Son. He who has the Son has life.

John 10:27–29
Jesus said, "My sheep listen to my voice; I know
them, and they follow me. I give them eternal life,
and they shall never perish; no one can snatch
them out of my hand. My Father, who has given
them to me, is greater than all; no one can snatch
them out of my Father's hand."

John 6:47
He who believes has everlasting life.

Romans 10:9–10
If you confess with your mouth, "Jesus is Lord," and believe in your heart that God raised him from the dead, you will be saved. For it is with your heart that you believe and are justified, and it is with your mouth that you confess and are saved.

John 11:25–26
Jesus said, "I am the resurrection and the life. He who believes in me will live, even though he dies; and whoever lives and believes in me will never die."

Hebrews 9:28
Christ was sacrificed once to take away the sins of many people; and he will appear a second time, not to bear sin, but to bring salvation to those who are waiting for him.

John 14:2–3

Jesus said, "In my Father's house are many rooms ... I am going there to prepare a place for you. And if I go and prepare a place for you, I will come back and take you to be with me that you also may be where I am."

2 Corinthians 5:1

We know that if the earthly tent we live in is destroyed, we have a building from God, an eternal house in heaven, not built by human hands.

Revelation 21:27

Nothing impure will ever enter the Holy City, ... but only those whose names are written in the Lamb's book of life.

Luke 10:20

Rejoice that your names are written in heaven.

Revelation 21:1, 3-4

I saw a new heaven and a new earth, for the first heaven and the first earth had passed away, and there was no longer any sea. ... And I heard a loud voice from the throne saying, "Now the dwelling of God is with men, and he will live with them. They will be his people, and God himself will be with them and be their God. He will wipe every tear from their eyes. There will be no more death or mourning or crying or pain, for the old order of things has passed away."

Revelation 7:16-17

Never again will they hunger;

    never again will they thirst.

The sun will not beat upon them,

    nor any scorching heat.

For the Lamb at the center of the throne will be their shepherd; he will lead them to springs of living water.

And God will wipe away every tear from their eyes.

Acts 3:19

Repent, then, and turn to God, so that your sins
may be wiped out, that times of refreshing may
come from the Lord.

2 Peter 3:9

The Lord is not slow in keeping his promise, as
some understand slowness. He is patient with you,
not wanting anyone to perish, but everyone to
come to repentance.

My favorite verses about Eternal Life

_____

_____

_____

_____

_____

_____

_____

_____

_____

_____

_____

_____

_____

_____

_____

_____

_____

_____

_____

_____

Thoughts and Reflections about Eternal Life

_____

_____

_____

_____

_____

_____

_____

_____

_____

_____

_____

_____

_____

_____

_____

_____

_____

A Full Life on Earth

John 10:10
Jesus said, "I have come that [those who believe] may have life, and have it to the full."

Deuteronomy 30:20
Love the LORD your God, listen to his voice, and hold fast to him. For the LORD is your life.

John 6:35
Jesus declared, "I am the bread of life. He who comes to me will never go hungry, and he who believes in me will never be thirsty."

2 Corinthians 3:17
The Lord is the Spirit, and where the Spirit of the Lord is, there is freedom.

Romans 6:11
Count yourselves dead to sin but alive to God in
Christ Jesus.

Romans 8:2
Through Christ Jesus the law of the Spirit of life
set me free from the law of sin and death.

John 6:63
Jesus said, "The Spirit gives life; the flesh counts
for nothing. The words I have spoken to you are
spirit and they are life."

Romans 8:11
If the Spirit of God who raised Jesus from the dead
is living in you, he who raised Christ from the dead
will also give life to your mortal bodies through his
Spirit, who lives in you.

Job 33:4
The Spirit of God has made me;

the breath of the Almighty gives me life.

Proverbs 3:1–2
Do not forget my teaching,

     but keep my commands in your heart,
for they will prolong your life many years

     and bring you prosperity.

Luke 17:21
The kingdom of God is within you.

Romans 14:17
The kingdom of God is not a matter of eating and
drinking, but of righteousness, peace and joy in
the Holy Spirit.

Luke 12:32
Do not be afraid, little flock, for your Father has
been pleased to give you the kingdom.

Deuteronomy 5:33
Walk in all the way that the LORD your God has
commanded you, so that you may live and prosper
and prolong your days in the land that you will
possess.

1 Timothy 6:11–12
Pursue righteousness, godliness, faith, love, endurance and gentleness. Fight the good fight of the faith. Take hold of the eternal life to which you were called when you made your good confession in the presence of many witnesses.

Isaiah 30:21
Whether you turn to the right or to the left, your ears will hear a voice behind you, saying, "This is the way; walk in it."

Psalm 36:7–10
How priceless is your unfailing love, O Lord!
Both high and low among men
> find refuge in the shadow of your wings.
They feast on the abundance of your house;
> you give them drink from your river of delights.
For with you is the fountain of life;
> in your light we see light.
Continue your love to those who know you,
> your righteousness to the upright in heart.

My favorite verses about a full life on earth

_____
_____
_____
_____
_____
_____
_____
_____
_____
_____
_____
_____
_____
_____
_____
_____
_____

Thoughts and Reflections about a full life on earth

_____

_____

_____

_____

_____

_____

_____

_____

_____

_____

_____

_____

_____

_____

Plans for the Future

Jeremiah 29:11–13

"I know the plans I have for you," declares the
LORD, "plans to prosper you and not to harm you,
plans to give you hope and a future. Then you will
call upon me and come and pray to me, and I will
listen to you. You will seek me and find me when
you seek me with all your heart."

1 Corinthians 2:9–10

As it is written:

"No eye has seen,

   no ear has heard,

no mind has conceived

   what God has prepared
   for those who love him"—

but God has revealed it to us by his Spirit. The
Spirit searches all things, even the deep things of
God.

Psalm 37:4
Delight yourself in the LORD

    and he will give you the desires of your heart.

Philippians 1:6
God who began a good work in you will carry it on
to completion until the day of Christ Jesus.

Psalm 138:8
The LORD will fulfill his purpose for me;

    your love, O LORD, endures forever—

    do not abandon the works of your hands.

1 John 3:2
Dear friends, now we are children of God, and
what we will be has not yet been made known.
But we know that when he appears, we shall be
like him, for we shall see him as he is.

Psalm 33:11

The plans of the LORD stand firm forever,

the purposes of his heart through all generations.

John 16:33

Jesus said, "I have told you these things, so that in me you may have peace. In this world you will have trouble. But take heart! I have overcome the world."

Matthew 6:20–21

Store up for yourselves treasures in heaven, where moth and rust do not destroy, and where thieves do not break in and steal. For where your treasure is, there your heart will be also.

Matthew 6:33–34
Seek first God's kingdom and his righteousness,
and all these things will be given to you as well.
Therefore do not worry about tomorrow, for
tomorrow will worry about itself. Each day has
enough trouble of its own.

Isaiah 43:18–19
"Forget the former things;

do not dwell on the past.
See, I am doing a new thing!

Now it springs up; do you not perceive it?
I am making a way in the desert

and streams in the wasteland.

Ezekiel 36:26
God said, "I will give you a new heart and put a
new spirit in you; I will remove from you your
heart of stone and give you a heart of flesh."

Malachi 3:10
"Bring the whole tithe into the storehouse, that there may be food in my house. Test me in this," says the LORD Almighty, "and see if I will not throw open the floodgates of heaven and pour out so much blessing that you will not have room enough for it."

Joshua 1:7
God said, "Be strong and very courageous. Be careful to obey all the law my servant Moses gave you; do not turn from it to the right or to the left, that you may be successful wherever you go."

Proverbs 16:3
Commit to the LORD whatever you do,
    and your plans will succeed.

Psalm 20:4
May the LORD give you the desire of your heart
    and make all your plans succeed.

Proverbs 13:4
The desires of the diligent are fully satisfied.

Psalm 1:1–3

Blessed is the man

    who does not walk in the counsel of the wicked

or stand in the way of sinners

    or sit in the seat of mockers.

His delight is in the law of the LORD,

    and on his law he meditates day and night.

He is like a tree planted by streams of water,

    which yields its fruit in season

and whose leaf does not wither.

    Whatever he does prospers.

Zechariah 4:6

"Not by might nor by power, but by my Spirit,"
says the LORD Almighty.

1 Corinthians 15:58

Stand firm. Let nothing move you. Always give
yourselves fully to the work of the Lord, because
you know that your labor in the Lord is not in vain.

My favorite verses about plans for the future

_____

_____

_____

_____

_____

_____

_____

_____

_____

_____

_____

_____

_____

_____

_____

_____

_____

Thoughts and Reflections about plans for the future

_____

_____

_____

_____

_____

_____

_____

_____

_____

_____

_____

_____

_____

_____

_____

_____

Wait for God and He Will Provide

Lamentations 3:24
The LORD is my portion;

therefore I will wait for him.

Lamentations 3:26
It is good to wait quietly

for the salvation of the LORD.

Psalm 5:3
In the morning, O LORD, you hear my voice;

in the morning I lay my requests before you

and wait in expectation.

Psalm 27:14
Wait for the LORD;

be strong and take heart

and wait for the LORD.

Isaiah 30:18

The LORD longs to be gracious to you;

> he rises to show you compassion.

For the LORD is a God of justice.

> Blessed are all who wait for him!

Psalm 33:20

We wait in hope for the LORD;

> he is our help and our shield.

Psalm 38:15

I wait for you, O LORD;

> you will answer, O Lord my God.

Psalm 119:166

I wait for your salvation, O LORD,

> and I follow your commands.

Psalm 130:5–6

I wait for the LORD, my soul waits,

and in his word I put my hope.

My soul waits for the LORD

more than watchmen wait for the morning.

Isaiah 26:8

Yes, LORD, walking in the way of your laws,

we wait for you;

your name and renown

are the desire of our hearts.

Isaiah 51:5

"My righteousness draws near speedily,

my salvation is on the way,

and my arm will bring justice to the nations.

The islands will look to me

and wait in hope for my arm."

declares the LORD.

Isaiah 64:4

Since ancient times no one has heard,

no ear has perceived,

no eye has seen any God besides you,

who acts on behalf of those who wait for him.

Micah 7:7

I watch in hope for the LORD,

I wait for God my Savior;

my God will hear me.

Romans 8:25

If we hope for what we do not yet have, we wait
for it patiently.

1 Corinthians 1:7

You do not lack any spiritual gift as you eagerly
wait for our Lord Jesus Christ to be revealed.

1 Corinthians 4:5

Judge nothing before the appointed time; wait till the Lord comes. He will bring to light what is hidden in darkness and will expose the motives of men's hearts. At that time each will receive his praise from God.

Jude 1:21

Keep yourselves in God's love as you wait for the mercy of our Lord Jesus Christ to bring you to eternal life.

John 16:33

Jesus said, "I have told you these things, so that in me you may have peace. In this world you will have trouble. But take heart! I have overcome the world."

Psalm 60:12

With God we will gain the victory,

and he will trample down our enemies.

Hosea 6:3

Let us acknowledge the LORD;

> let us press on to acknowledge him.

As surely as the sun rises,

> he will appear;

he will come to us like the winter rains,

> like the spring rains that water the earth.

Psalm 40:1–2

I waited patiently for the LORD;

> he turned to me and heard my cry.

He lifted me out of the slimy pit,

> out of the mud and mire;

he set my feet on a rock

> and gave me a firm place to stand.

My favorite verses about waiting for God

_____

_____

_____

_____

_____

_____

_____

_____

_____

_____

_____

_____

_____

_____

_____

_____

_____

Thoughts and Reflections about waiting for God

_____

_____

_____

_____

_____

_____

_____

_____

_____

_____

_____

_____

_____

_____

_____

_____

_____

_____

God Hears Your Prayers

Jeremiah 29:12
"You will call upon me and come and pray to me,
and I will listen to you," declares the LORD.

Psalm 66:19–20
God has surely listened

and heard my voice in prayer.

Praise be to God,

who has not rejected my prayer

or withheld his love from me!

2 Chronicles 6:40
Now, my God, may your eyes be open and your
ears attentive to the prayers offered in this place.

Psalm 34:17
The righteous cry out, and the LORD hears them;

he delivers them from all their troubles.

Psalm 69:33
The LORD hears the needy

and does not despise his captive people.

Hebrews 5:7
During the days of Jesus' life on earth, he offered up prayers and petitions with loud cries and tears to the one who could save him from death, and he was heard because of his reverent submission.

2 Chronicles 7:14
God said, "If my people, who are called by my name, will humble themselves and pray and seek my face and turn from their wicked ways, then will I hear from heaven and will forgive their sin and will heal their land."

Psalm 65:2
O you, LORD, who hear prayer,

to you all men will come.

Proverbs 15:8
The prayer of the upright pleases God.

Proverbs 15:29
God hears the prayer of the righteous.

Romans 8:26
The Spirit helps us in our weakness. We do not
know what we ought to pray for, but the Spirit
himself intercedes for us with groans that words
cannot express.

Philippians 4:6–7
Do not be anxious about anything, but in everything, by prayer and petition, with thanksgiving,
present your requests to God. And the peace of
God, which transcends all understanding, will
guard your hearts and your minds in Christ Jesus.

James 5:13
Is any one of you in trouble? He should pray. Is
anyone happy? Let him sing songs of praise.

1 Peter 3:12

The eyes of the Lord are on the righteous

and his ears are attentive to their prayer.

Psalm 4:3

The LORD will hear when I call to him.

Psalm 31:22

In my alarm I said,

"I am cut off from your sight!"

Yet you heard my cry for mercy, O LORD,

when I called to you for help.

My favorite verses about God hearing my prayers

_____
_____
_____
_____
_____
_____
_____
_____
_____
_____
_____
_____
_____
_____
_____
_____
_____
_____

Thoughts and Reflections about God hearing my prayers

_____

_____

_____

_____

_____

_____

_____

_____

_____

_____

_____

_____

_____

_____

God Answers Your Prayers

James 5:15–16

The prayer offered in faith will make the sick person well; the Lord will raise him up. If he has sinned, he will be forgiven. Therefore confess your sins to each other and pray for each other so that you may be healed. The prayer of a righteous man is powerful and effective.

Matthew 21:22

If you believe, you will receive whatever you ask for in prayer.

Jeremiah 31:9

"My people will come with weeping;

they will pray as I bring them back.

I will lead them beside streams of water

on a level path where they will not stumble.

Psalm 102:17

The LORD will respond to the prayer of the destitute;

   he will not despise their plea.

Psalm 6:9

The LORD has heard my cry for mercy;

   the LORD accepts my prayer.

Psalm 17:6

I call on you, O God, for you will answer me;

   give ear to me and hear my prayer.

Deuteronomy 4:7

The LORD our God is near us whenever we pray to him.

Matthew 17:20

Jesus said, "If you have faith as small as a mustard seed, you can say to this mountain, 'Move from here to there' and it will move. Nothing will be impossible for you."

Mark 11:24
Whatever you ask for in prayer, believe that you have received it, and it will be yours.

Daniel 9:23
The angel Gabriel said to Daniel, "As soon as you began to pray, an answer was given, which I have come to tell you, for you are highly esteemed."

2 Chronicles 32:24
Hezekiah became ill and was at the point of death. He prayed to the LORD, who answered him and gave him a miraculous sign.

James 5:17–18
Elijah was a man just like us. He prayed earnestly that it would not rain, and it did not rain on the land for three and a half years. Again he prayed, and the heavens gave rain, and the earth produced its crops.

Acts 12:5–7, 9–11

Peter was kept in prison, but the church was earnestly praying to God for him.

The night before Herod was to bring him to trial, Peter was sleeping between two soldiers, bound with two chains, and sentries stood guard at the entrance. Suddenly an angel of the Lord appeared and a light shone in the cell. He struck Peter on the side and woke him up. "Quick, get up!" he said, and the chains fell off Peter's wrists. . . .

Peter followed [the angel] out of the prison, but he had no idea that what the angel was doing was really happening; he thought he was seeing a vision. They passed the first and second guards and came to the iron gate leading to the city. It opened for them by itself, and they went through it. When they had walked the length of one street, suddenly the angel left him.

Then Peter came to himself and said, "Now I know without a doubt that the Lord sent his angel and rescued me. . . ."

My favorite verses about
God answering my prayers

_____
_____
_____
_____
_____
_____
_____
_____
_____
_____
_____
_____
_____
_____
_____
_____
_____
_____
_____

Thoughts and Reflections about God answering my prayers

_____

_____

_____

_____

_____

_____

_____

_____

_____

_____

_____

_____

_____

_____

_____

Finding God's Will

Jeremiah 29:13
"You will seek me and find me when you seek me with all your heart," declares the LORD.

Romans 12:2
Do not conform any longer to the pattern of this world, but be transformed by the renewing of your mind. Then you will be able to test and approve what God's will is—his good, pleasing and perfect will.

Colossians 1:9
Since the day we heard about you, we have not stopped praying for you and asking God to fill you with the knowledge of his will through all spiritual wisdom and understanding.

1 Thessalonians 5:18
Give thanks in all circumstances, for this is God's will for you in Christ Jesus.

1 John 2:17
The world and its desires pass away, but the man who does the will of God lives forever.

1 Peter 2:15
It is God's will that by doing good you should silence the ignorant talk of foolish men.

Mark 3:35
Jesus said, "Whoever does God's will is my brother and sister and mother."

John 9:31
God listens to the godly man who does his will.

Ephesians 1:9
God made known to us the mystery of his will according to his good pleasure, which he purposed in Christ.

Ephesians 1:11

In Christ we were also chosen, having been pre-destined according to the plan of God who works out everything in conformity with the purpose of his will.

1 Thessalonians 4:3

It is God's will that you should be sanctified.

1 John 5:14

This is the confidence we have in approaching God: that if we ask anything according to his will, he hears us.

Jeremiah 6:16

This is what the LORD says:

   "Stand at the crossroads and look;
ask for the ancient paths,

   ask where the good way is, and walk in it,
and you will find rest for your souls."

James 1:5

If any of you lacks wisdom, he should ask God,
who gives generously to all without finding fault,
and it will be given to him.

Jeremiah 33:3

"Call to me and I will answer you and tell you
great and unsearchable things you do not know,"
says the LORD.

John 14:16–17

Jesus said, "I will ask the Father, and he will give
you another Counselor to be with you forever—the
Spirit of truth. The world cannot accept him,
because it neither sees him nor knows him. But you
know him, for he lives with you and will be in you."

Proverbs 3:5–6

Trust in the LORD with all your heart

   and lean not on your own understanding;

in all your ways acknowledge him,

   and he will make your paths straight.

Proverbs 16:9

In his heart a man plans his course,

but the LORD determines his steps.

Psalm 37:23-24
If the LORD delights in a man's way,

he makes his steps firm;

though he stumble, he will not fall,

for the LORD upholds him with his hand.

Psalm 37:4
Delight yourself in the LORD

and he will give you the desires of your heart.

Philippians 3:13-14
One thing I do: Forgetting what is behind and straining toward what is ahead, I press on toward the goal to win the prize for which God has called me heavenward in Christ Jesus.

1 Corinthians 2:16
"Who has known the mind of the Lord

that he may instruct him?"
But we have the mind of Christ.

Romans 8:27–28
God who searches our hearts knows the mind of
the Spirit, because the Spirit intercedes for the
saints in accordance with God's will. And we know
that in all things God works for the good of those
who love him, who have been called according to
his purpose.

My favorite verses about finding God's Will

_____

_____

_____

_____

_____

_____

_____

_____

_____

_____

_____

_____

_____

_____

_____

_____

_____

Thoughts and Reflections about finding God's Will

_____

_____

_____

_____

_____

_____

_____

_____

_____

_____

_____

_____

_____

_____

_____

_____

_____

_____

Chapter Four

What Does God Provide in Times of Need?

Promises about the Fruit of the Spirit

Thank you, Lord Jesus, for
your generous provision.
Thank you that when I
invited you into my life,
you made my heart your
dwelling place. Because your
Spirit lives within me, you
empower me to bear the
fruit of the Spirit.

Love

1 Corinthians 13:4–6
Love is patient, love is kind. It does not envy, it does not boast, it is not proud. It is not rude, it is not self-seeking, it is not easily angered, it keeps no record of wrongs. Love does not delight in evil but rejoices with the truth.

2 Timothy 1:7
God did not give us a spirit of timidity, but a spirit of power, of love and of self-discipline.

1 Peter 4:8
Above all, love each other deeply, because love covers over a multitude of sins.

1 John 4:19
We love because God first loved us.

Ephesians 5:2
Live a life of love, just as Christ loved us and gave himself up for us as a fragrant offering and sacrifice to God.

Luke 6:35
Love your enemies, do good to them, and lend to them without expecting to get anything back. Then your reward will be great, and you will be sons of the Most High.

John 13:34–35
Jesus said, "Love one another. As I have loved you, so you must love one another. By this all men will know that you are my disciples, if you love one another."

John 14:21
Jesus said, "Whoever has my commands and obeys them, he is the one who loves me. He who loves me will be loved by my Father, and I too will love him and show myself to him."

Romans 8:28
We know that in all things God works for the good of those who love him, who have been called according to his purpose.

1 Corinthians 13:8
Love never fails.

1 Corinthians 13:13
These three remain: faith, hope and love. But the greatest of these is love.

Ephesians 3:17–19
I pray that you, being rooted and established in love, may have power, together with all the saints, to grasp how wide and long and high and deep is the love of Christ, and to know this love that surpasses knowledge—that you may be filled to the measure of all the fullness of God.

Ephesians 6:24
Grace to all who love our Lord Jesus Christ with an undying love.

1 Thessalonians 3:12
May the Lord make your love increase and over-flow for each other and for everyone else.

Hebrews 10:24
Let us consider how we may spur one another on toward love and good deeds.

1 Peter 1:22
Now that you have purified yourselves by obeying the truth so that you have sincere love for your brothers, love one another deeply, from the heart.

1 John 4:7
Dear friends, let us love one another, for love comes from God. Everyone who loves has been born of God and knows God.

1 John 4:16

We know and rely on the love God has for us. God is love. Whoever lives in love lives in God, and God in him.

Romans 13:8

Let no debt remain outstanding, except the continuing debt to love one another, for he who loves his fellowman has fulfilled the law.

Proverbs 17:9

He who covers over an offense promotes love,

but whoever repeats the matter separates close friends.

Deuteronomy 33:3

Surely it is you, LORD, who love the people;

all the holy ones are in your hand.

At your feet they all bow down,

and from you receive instruction.

Deuteronomy 33:12

Let the beloved of the LORD rest secure in him,

for he shields him all day long,

and the one the LORD loves rests
between his shoulders.

Psalm 23:6

Surely goodness and love will follow me

all the days of my life,

and I will dwell in the house of the LORD

forever.

My favorite verses about love

_____

_____

_____

_____

_____

_____

_____

_____

_____

_____

_____

_____

_____

_____

_____

_____

_____

_____

Thoughts and Reflections about love

_____

_____

_____

_____

_____

_____

_____

_____

_____

_____

_____

_____

_____

_____

_____

_____

_____

_____

_____

Joy

Nehemiah 8:10
The joy of the LORD is your strength.

Job 8:21
God will yet fill your mouth with laughter

and your lips with shouts of joy.

Isaiah 55:12
You will go out in joy

and be led forth in peace;

the mountains and hills

will burst into song before you,

and all the trees of the field

will clap their hands.

Psalm 97:11
Light is shed upon the righteous

and joy on the upright in heart.

Psalm 63:3–5

Because your love is better than life, O LORD,

> my lips will glorify you.

I will praise you as long as I live,

> and in your name I will lift up my hands.

My soul will be satisfied

> as with the richest of foods;

> with singing lips my mouth will praise you.

Psalm 119:111

Your statutes are my heritage forever, O LORD;

> they are the joy of my heart.

Proverbs 15:30

A cheerful look brings joy to the heart,

> and good news gives health to the bones.

Psalm 92:4

You make me glad by your deeds, O LORD;

> I sing for joy at the works of your hands.

Isaiah 51:11

The ransomed of the LORD will return.

> They will enter Zion with singing;
>
> everlasting joy will crown their heads.

Gladness and joy will overtake them,

> and sorrow and sighing will flee away.

Joel 2:23

Be glad, O people of Zion,

> rejoice in the LORD your God,

for he has given you

> the autumn rains in righteousness.

He sends you abundant showers,

> both autumn and spring rains, as before.

Psalm 19:8

The precepts of the LORD are right,

> giving joy to the heart.

The commands of the LORD are radiant,

> giving light to the eyes.

Luke 6:22–23

Blessed are you when men hate you,

when they exclude you and insult you

and reject your name as evil,

because of the Son of Man.

Rejoice in that day and leap for joy, because great
is your reward in heaven. For that is how their
fathers treated the prophets.

Psalm 30:11–12

You turned my wailing into dancing;

you removed my sackcloth
and clothed me with joy,

that my heart may sing to you and not be silent.

O LORD my God, I will give you thanks forever.

Psalm 5:11

Let all who take refuge in you be glad, O LORD;

let them ever sing for joy.

1 Peter 1:8–9

Though you have not seen Jesus, you love him;
and even though you do not see him now, you
believe in him and are filled with an inexpressible
and glorious joy, for you are receiving the goal of
your faith, the salvation of your souls.

John 16:24

Jesus said, "Until now you have not asked for anything in my name. Ask and you will receive, and
your joy will be complete."

Job 33:26, 28

[A person] prays to God and finds favor with him,

he sees God's face and shouts for joy;

he is restored by God to his righteous state. ...

Then he ... says, "God redeemed my soul from
going down to the pit,

and I will live to enjoy the light."

Psalm 13:5–6

I trust in your unfailing love, O LORD;

my heart rejoices in your salvation.

I will sing to the LORD,

for he has been good to me.

Psalm 16:11

You have made known to me
the path of life, O LORD;

you will fill me with joy in your presence,

with eternal pleasures at your right hand.

My favorite verses about joy

_____

_____

_____

_____

_____

_____

_____

_____

_____

_____

_____

_____

_____

_____

_____

_____

_____

_____

Thoughts and Reflections about joy

_____

_____

_____

_____

_____

_____

_____

_____

_____

_____

_____

_____

_____

_____

_____

_____

_____

_____

_____

Patience and Perseverance

Psalm 40:1

I waited patiently for the LORD;

he turned to me and heard my cry.

Psalm 37:7

Be still before the LORD and wait patiently for him.

Proverbs 19:11

A man's wisdom gives him patience;

it is to his glory to overlook an offense.

Proverbs 12:16

A prudent man overlooks an insult.

Psalm 27:14

Wait for the LORD;

be strong and take heart

and wait for the LORD.

Ecclesiastes 7:8
The end of a matter is better than its beginning,
    and patience is better than pride.

Lamentations 3:26
It is good to wait quietly
    for the salvation of the LORD.

Romans 5:3–4
We also rejoice in our sufferings, because we know
that suffering produces perseverance; perseverance, character; and character, hope.

James 1:2–4
Consider it pure joy, my brothers, whenever you
face trials of many kinds, because you know that
the testing of your faith develops perseverance.
Perseverance must finish its work so that you may
be mature and complete, not lacking anything.

Romans 8:25
If we hope for what we do not yet have, we wait for it patiently.

Colossians 1:10–11
We pray ... that you may live a life worthy of the Lord and may please him in every way: bearing fruit in every good work, growing in the knowledge of God, being strengthened with all power according to his glorious might so that you may have great endurance and patience.

1 Timothy 1:16
I was shown mercy so that in me, the worst of sinners, Christ Jesus might display his unlimited patience as an example for those who would believe on him and receive eternal life.

Hebrews 10:36
You need to persevere so that when you have done the will of God, you will receive what he has promised.

Galatians 6:9
Let us not become weary in doing good, for at the proper time we will reap a harvest if we do not give up.

James 5:7–8
See how the farmer waits for the land to yield its valuable crop and how patient he is for the autumn and spring rains. You too, be patient and stand firm, because the Lord's coming is near.

2 Peter 3:9
The Lord is not slow in keeping his promise, as some understand slowness. He is patient with you, not wanting anyone to perish, but everyone to come to repentance.

Psalm 130:5–6
I wait for the LORD, my soul waits,

and in his word I put my hope.

My soul waits for the LORD

more than watchmen wait for the morning.

Proverbs 14:29
A patient man has great understanding.

2 Corinthians 1:6–7
If we are distressed, it is for your comfort and salvation; if we are comforted, it is for your comfort, which produces in you patient endurance of the same sufferings we suffer. And our hope for you is firm, because we know that just as you share in our sufferings, so also you share in our comfort.

James 5:10–11
As an example of patience in the face of suffering, take the prophets who spoke in the name of the Lord. As you know, we consider blessed those who have persevered. You have heard of Job's perseverance and have seen what the Lord finally brought about. The Lord is full of compassion and mercy.

Revelation 3:10–12

Jesus says, "Since you have kept my command to endure patiently, I will also keep you from the hour of trial that is going to come upon the whole world to test those who live on the earth.

I am coming soon. Hold on to what you have, so that no one will take your crown. Him who overcomes I will make a pillar in the temple of my God. Never again will he leave it. I will write on him the name of my God and the name of the city of my God, the new Jerusalem, which is coming down out of heaven from my God; and I will also write on him my new name."

My favorite verses about patience and perseverance

_____

_____

_____

_____

_____

_____

_____

_____

_____

_____

_____

_____

_____

_____

_____

_____

_____

_____

_____

Thoughts and Reflections about patience and perseverance

_____

_____

_____

_____

_____

_____

_____

_____

_____

_____

_____

_____

_____

_____

_____

_____

Peace

Romans 8:6
The mind controlled by the Spirit is life and peace.

Isaiah 26:3
You will keep in perfect peace

him whose mind is steadfast,

because he trusts in you, O LORD.

John 14:27
Jesus said, "Peace I leave with you; my peace I give you. I do not give to you as the world gives. Do not let your hearts be troubled and do not be afraid."

Romans 5:1
Since we have been justified through faith, we have peace with God through our Lord Jesus Christ.

Psalm 85:8

I will listen to what God the LORD will say;

>he promises peace to his people, his saints.

Psalm 119:165

Great peace have they who love your law, O LORD

>and nothing can make them stumble.

Philippians 4:6–7

In everything, by prayer and petition, with thanksgiving, present your requests to God. And the peace of God, which transcends all understanding, will guard your hearts and your minds in Christ Jesus.

Proverbs 16:7

When a man's ways are pleasing to the LORD,

>he makes even his enemies live at peace with him.

Matthew 5:9
Blessed are the peacemakers,

for they will be called sons of God.

2 Corinthians 13:11
Aim for perfection, listen to my appeal, be of one
mind, live in peace. And the God of love and peace
will be with you.

Psalm 4:8
I will lie down and sleep in peace,

for you alone, O Lord,

make me dwell in safety.

Psalm 23:1–4

The LORD is my shepherd, I shall not be in want.

He makes me lie down in green pastures,

he leads me beside quiet waters,

he restores my soul.

He guides me in paths of righteousness

for his name's sake.

Even though I walk

through the valley of the shadow of death,

I will fear no evil,

for you are with me;

your rod and your staff,

they comfort me.

Psalm 29:11

The LORD gives strength to his people;

the LORD blesses his people with peace.

Psalm 62:1
My soul finds rest in God alone;

 my salvation comes from him.

Proverbs 14:30
A heart at peace gives life to the body.

Isaiah 26:12
LORD, you establish peace for us;

 all that we have accomplished you have done
for us.

Matthew 11:28
Jesus said, "Come to me, all you who are weary
and burdened, and I will give you rest."

Ephesians 2:17
Jesus came and preached peace to you who were
far away and peace to those who were near.

John 20:21
Jesus said, "Peace be with you! As the Father has sent me, I am sending you."

James 3:17–18
The wisdom that comes from heaven is first of all pure; then peace-loving, considerate, submissive, full of mercy and good fruit, impartial and sincere. Peacemakers who sow in peace raise a harvest of righteousness.

1 Peter 5:7
Cast all your anxiety on God because he cares for you.

My favorite verses about peace

_____

_____

_____

_____

_____

_____

_____

_____

_____

_____

_____

_____

_____

_____

_____

_____

_____

Thoughts and Reflections about peace

_____

_____

_____

_____

_____

_____

_____

_____

_____

_____

_____

_____

_____

_____

_____

_____

Hope

Lamentations 3:21, 25–26

This I call to mind

and therefore I have hope: …

The LORD is good to those whose hope is in him,

to the one who seeks him;

it is good to wait quietly

for the salvation of the LORD.

Psalm 71:5

You have been my hope, O Sovereign LORD,

my confidence since my youth.

Isaiah 40:31

Those who hope in the LORD

will renew their strength.

They will soar on wings like eagles;

they will run and not grow weary,

they will walk and not be faint.

Romans 5:2–5
We rejoice in the hope of the glory of God. Not only so, but we also rejoice in our sufferings, because we know that suffering produces perseverance; perseverance, character; and character, hope. And hope does not disappoint us, because God has poured out his love into our hearts by the Holy Spirit, whom he has given us.

1 Timothy 4:10
We have put our hope in the living God, who is the Savior of all men, and especially of those who believe.

1 Peter 1:3
Praise be to the God and Father of our Lord Jesus Christ! In his great mercy he has given us new birth into a living hope through the resurrection of Jesus Christ from the dead.

1 Peter 1:21

Through Jesus you believe in God, who raised him
from the dead and glorified him, and so your faith
and hope are in God.

Acts 2:26–27

My heart is glad and my tongue rejoices;

my body also will live in hope,

because you will not abandon me to the grave,

nor will you let your Holy One see decay.

Psalm 147:11

The LORD delights in those who fear him,

who put their hope in his unfailing love.

Proverbs 24:14

Know also that wisdom is sweet to your soul;

if you find it, there is a future hope for you,

and your hope will not be cut off.

Psalm 42:11

Why are you downcast, O my soul?

Why so disturbed within me?

Put your hope in God,

for I will yet praise him,

my Savior and my God.

Psalm 119:114

You are my refuge and my shield, O LORD;

I have put my hope in your word.

Romans 15:13

May the God of hope fill you with all joy and
peace as you trust in him, so that you may over-
flow with hope by the power of the Holy Spirit.

2 Thessalonians 2:16–17

May our Lord Jesus Christ himself and God our Father, who loved us and by his grace gave us eternal encouragement and good hope, encourage your hearts and strengthen you in every good deed and word.

Hebrews 6:17–19

Because God wanted to make the unchanging nature of his purpose very clear to the heirs of what was promised, he confirmed it with an oath. God did this so that, by two unchangeable things in which it is impossible for God to lie, we who have fled to take hold of the hope offered to us may be greatly encouraged. We have this hope as an anchor for the soul, firm and secure.

1 Peter 1:13

Set your hope fully on the grace to be given you when Jesus Christ is revealed.

1 John 3:3
Everyone who has this hope in him purifies himself, just as Christ is pure.

Titus 3:4–7
When the kindness and love of God our Savior
appeared, he saved us, not because of righteous
things we had done, but because of his mercy. He
saved us through the washing of rebirth and
renewal by the Holy Spirit, whom he poured out on
us generously through Jesus Christ our Savior, so
that, having been justified by his grace, we might
become heirs having the hope of eternal life.

My favorite verses about hope

_____
_____
_____
_____
_____
_____
_____
_____
_____
_____
_____
_____
_____
_____
_____
_____
_____

Thoughts and
Reflections about hope

_____

_____

_____

_____

_____

_____

_____

_____

_____

_____

_____

_____

_____

_____

_____

_____

_____

_____

Chapter Five

What Does God Give to His Children?
Promises about God's Perfect Gifts for You

Thank you, God, that you have adopted me as your very own child. You know my every need and desire, and you give me perfect gifts. Thank you, my good Father, that you want more for me than even I want for myself.

Amazing Grace

Ephesians 2:8-10
It is by grace you have been saved, through faith—
and this not from yourselves, it is the gift of God—
not by works, so that no one can boast. For we are
God's workmanship, created in Christ Jesus to do
good works, which God prepared in advance for us
to do.

Psalm 116:5
The LORD is gracious and righteous;
    our God is full of compassion.

Ephesians 2:6–7
God raised us up with Christ and seated us with
him in the heavenly realms in Christ Jesus, in order
that in the coming ages he might show the
incomparable riches of his grace, expressed in his
kindness to us in Christ Jesus.

Romans 5:1–2

Since we have been justified through faith, we have peace with God through our Lord Jesus Christ, through whom we have gained access by faith into this grace in which we now stand. And we rejoice in the hope of the glory of God.

Romans 5:17

If, by the trespass of the one man, death reigned through that one man, how much more will those who receive God's abundant provision of grace and of the gift of righteousness reign in life through the one man, Jesus Christ.

2 Corinthians 8:9

You know the grace of our Lord Jesus Christ, that though he was rich, yet for your sakes he became poor, so that you through his poverty might become rich.

John 1:16

From the fullness of God's grace we have all received one blessing after another.

2 Corinthians 9:8

God is able to make all grace abound to you, so that in all things at all times, having all that you need, you will abound in every good work.

2 Corinthians 12:9

The Lord said to me, "My grace is sufficient for you, for my power is made perfect in weakness." Therefore I will boast all the more gladly about my weaknesses, so that Christ's power may rest on me.

1 Peter 5:10

The God of all grace, who called you to his eternal glory in Christ, after you have suffered a little while, will himself restore you and make you strong, firm and steadfast.

2 Peter 1:2

Grace and peace be yours in abundance through the knowledge of God and of Jesus our Lord.

Psalm 145:8

The LORD is gracious and compassionate,

slow to anger and rich in love.

Ephesians 1:5-7

God predestined us to be adopted as his sons through Jesus Christ, in accordance with his pleasure and will—to the praise of his glorious grace, which he has freely given us in the One he loves. In him we have redemption through his blood, the forgiveness of sins, in accordance with the riches of God's grace.

Hebrews 4:16

Let us ... approach the throne of grace with confidence, so that we may receive mercy and find grace to help us in our time of need.

James 4:6

God gives us more grace.

My favorite verses about Amazing Grace

_____

_____

_____

_____

_____

_____

_____

_____

_____

_____

_____

_____

_____

_____

_____

_____

_____

_____

Thoughts and Reflections about Amazing Grace

_____

_____

_____

_____

_____

_____

_____

_____

_____

_____

_____

_____

_____

_____

_____

_____

A Sense of Belonging

Isaiah 43:1

This is what the LORD says—

> he who created you, O Jacob,
>
> he who formed you, O Israel:

"Fear not, for I have redeemed you;

> I have summoned you by name; you are mine."

Jeremiah 31:3

The LORD appeared to us in the past, saying:

"I have loved you with an everlasting love;

> I have drawn you with loving-kindness."

Psalm 100:3

Know that the LORD is God.

> It is he who made us, and we are his;
>
> we are his people, the sheep of his pasture.

Isaiah 49:15–16

"Can a mother forget the baby at her breast

and have no compassion
on the child she has borne?

Though she may forget,

I will not forget you!

See, I have engraved you

on the palms of my hands;

your walls are ever before me,"

declares the LORD.

1 Samuel 12:22

For the sake of his great name the LORD will not reject his people, because the LORD was pleased to make you his own.

1 Peter 2:9

You are a chosen people, a royal priesthood, a holy nation, a people belonging to God, that you may declare the praises of him who called you out of darkness into his wonderful light.

Psalm 95:6–7

Come, let us bow down in worship,

let us kneel before the LORD our Maker;

for he is our God

and we are the people of his pasture,

the flock under his care.

Ephesians 1:13

You also were included in Christ when you heard the word of truth, the gospel of your salvation. Having believed, you were marked in him with a seal, the promised Holy Spirit.

Ephesians 2:10

We are God's workmanship, created in Christ Jesus to do good works, which God prepared in advance for us to do.

Colossians 3:12

As God's chosen people, holy and dearly loved, clothe yourselves with compassion, kindness, humility, gentleness and patience.

Philippians 3:20
Our citizenship is in heaven. And we eagerly await
a Savior from there, the Lord Jesus Christ.

Matthew 10:29–31
Are not two sparrows sold for a penny? Yet not
one of them will fall to the ground apart from the
will of your Father. And even the very hairs of your
head are all numbered. So don't be afraid; you are
worth more than many sparrows.

Psalm 139:13–14
O LORD, you created my inmost being;

> you knit me together in my mother's womb.

I praise you because I am

> fearfully and wonderfully made;

> your works are wonderful,

> I know that full well.

Ephesians 1:5–6

God predestined us to be adopted as his sons through Jesus Christ, in accordance with his pleasure and will—to the praise of his glorious grace, which he has freely given us in the One he loves.

Deuteronomy 7:6

You are a people holy to the LORD your God. The LORD your God has chosen you out of all the peoples on the face of the earth to be his people, his treasured possession.

Colossians 2:9–10

In Christ all the fullness of the Deity lives in bodily form, and you have been given fullness in Christ, who is the head over every power and authority.

1 Corinthians 12:27

You are the body of Christ, and each one of you is a part of it.

1 Thessalonians 5:5, 8–10

You are all sons of the light and sons of the day.
We do not belong to the night or to the darkness.
… But since we belong to the day, let us be self-
controlled, putting on faith and love as a breastplate, and the hope of salvation as a helmet. For
God did not appoint us to suffer wrath but to
receive salvation through our Lord Jesus Christ. He
died for us so that, whether we are awake or
asleep, we may live together with him.

My favorite verses about a Sense of Belonging

_____

_____

_____

_____

_____

_____

_____

_____

_____

_____

_____

_____

_____

_____

_____

_____

_____

_____

Thoughts and Reflections about a Sense of Belonging

_____

_____

_____

_____

_____

_____

_____

_____

_____

_____

_____

_____

_____

_____

_____

_____

Encouragement

2 Thessalonians 2:16–17
May our Lord Jesus Christ himself and God our
Father, who loved us and by his grace gave us
eternal encouragement and good hope, encourage
your hearts and strengthen you in every good
deed and word.

1 Thessalonians 5:11
Encourage one another and build each other up,
just as in fact you are doing.

Zephaniah 3:17
The LORD your God is with you,
    he is mighty to save.
He will take great delight in you,
    he will quiet you with his love,
    he will rejoice over you with singing.

John 14:16
Jesus said, "I will ask the Father, and he will give you another Counselor to be with you forever."

Psalm 10:17
You hear, O LORD, the desire of the afflicted;

> you encourage them,
> and you listen to their cry.

Lamentations 3:25–26
The LORD is good to those whose hope is in him,

> to the one who seeks him;

it is good to wait quietly

> for the salvation of the LORD.

Jeremiah 29:11
"I know the plans I have for you," declares the LORD, "plans to prosper you and not to harm you, plans to give you hope and a future."

Lamentations 3:22–23

Because of the LORD's great love
we are not consumed,

for his compassions never fail.

They are new every morning;

great is your faithfulness.

Psalm 68:19

Praise be to the LORD, to God our Savior,

who daily bears our burdens.

Psalm 55:22

Cast your cares on the LORD

and he will sustain you;

he will never let the righteous fall.

Galatians 6:9
Let us not become weary in doing good, for at the proper time we will reap a harvest if we do not give up.

Hebrews 6:10
God is not unjust; he will not forget your work and the love you have shown him as you have helped his people and continue to help them.

Romans 15:4–5
Everything that was written in the past was written to teach us, so that through endurance and the encouragement of the Scriptures we might have hope. May the God who gives endurance and encouragement give you a spirit of unity among yourselves as you follow Christ Jesus.

Philippians 1:6
God who began a good work in you will carry it on to completion until the day of Christ Jesus.

Philippians 4:6–7

Do not be anxious about anything, but in everything, by prayer and petition, with thanksgiving,
present your requests to God. And the peace of
God, which transcends all understanding, will
guard your hearts and your minds in Christ Jesus.

Psalm 23:1–4

The LORD is my shepherd, I shall not be in want.

　　He makes me lie down in green pastures,

he leads me beside quiet waters,

　　he restores my soul.

He guides me in paths of righteousness

　　for his name's sake.

Even though I walk

　　through the valley of the shadow of death,

I will fear no evil,

　　for you are with me, LORD;

your rod and your staff,

　　they comfort me.

John 14:1–3

Jesus said, "Do not let your hearts be troubled.
Trust in God; trust also in me. In my Father's house
are many rooms; if it were not so, I would have
told you. I am going there to prepare a place for
you. And if I go and prepare a place for you, I will
come back and take you to be with me that you
also may be where I am."

My favorite verses about encouragement

_____

_____

_____

_____

_____

_____

_____

_____

_____

_____

_____

_____

_____

_____

_____

_____

_____

_____

_____

Thoughts and Reflections about encouragement

_____

_____

_____

_____

_____

_____

_____

_____

_____

_____

_____

_____

_____

_____

_____

Contentment

Philippians 4:11–12
I have learned to be content whatever the circumstances. I know what it is to be in need, and I
know what it is to have plenty. I have learned the
secret of being content in any and every situation,
whether well fed or hungry, whether living in
plenty or in want.

Proverbs 19:23
The fear of the LORD leads to life:

Then one rests content, untouched by trouble.

1 Timothy 6:6–7
Godliness with contentment is great gain. For we
brought nothing into the world, and we can take
nothing out of it.

Psalm 16:2
I said to the LORD, "You are my LORD;

apart from you I have no good thing."

Ecclesiastes 2:24

A man can do nothing better than to eat and drink and find satisfaction in his work. This too, I see, is from the hand of God.

Psalm 103:5

The LORD satisfies your desires with good things

so that your youth is renewed like the eagle's.

Psalm 37:4

Delight yourself in the LORD

and he will give you the desires of your heart.

Psalm 107:8-9

Let them give thanks to the LORD

for his unfailing love

and his wonderful deeds for men,

for he satisfies the thirsty

and fills the hungry with good things.

Psalm 90:14

Satisfy us in the morning

with your unfailing love, O LORD,

that we may sing for joy

and be glad all our days.

Jeremiah 31:25

"I will refresh the weary and satisfy the faint," says the LORD.

Luke 6:21

Blessed are you who hunger now,

for you will be satisfied.

Blessed are you who weep now,

for you will laugh.

Psalm 91:16

"With long life will I satisfy him

and show him my salvation.,"

says the LORD.

Proverbs 15:15
The cheerful heart has a continual feast.

Psalm 46:10
"Be still, and know that I am God;

I will be exalted among the nations,

I will be exalted in the earth."

Psalm 107:28–30
They cried out to the LORD in their trouble,

and he brought them out of their distress.

He stilled the storm to a whisper;

the waves of the sea were hushed.

They were glad when it grew calm,

and he guided them to their desired haven.

Psalm 4:8
I will lie down and sleep in peace,

for you alone, O LORD,

make me dwell in safety.

Psalm 23:1-2

The LORD is my shepherd, I shall not be in want.

He makes me lie down in green pastures,

he leads me beside quiet waters.

Proverbs 1:33

Whoever listens to wisdom will live in safety

and be at ease, without fear of harm.

2 Peter 1:3

God's divine power has given us everything we need
for life and godliness through our knowledge of
him who called us by his own glory and goodness.

Philippians 4:19

My God will meet all your needs according to his
glorious riches in Christ Jesus.

2 Corinthians 9:8–11

God is able to make all grace abound to you, so that in all things at all times, having all that you need, you will abound in every good work. As it is written:

"He has scattered abroad his gifts to the poor; his righteousness endures forever."

Now he who supplies seed to the sower and bread for food will also supply and increase your store of seed and will enlarge the harvest of your righteousness. You will be made rich in every way so that you can be generous on every occasion, and through us your generosity will result in thanksgiving to God.

My favorite verses about contentment

_____

_____

_____

_____

_____

_____

_____

_____

_____

_____

_____

_____

_____

_____

_____

_____

_____

Thoughts and Reflections about contentment

_____

_____

_____

_____

_____

_____

_____

_____

_____

_____

_____

_____

_____

_____

_____

_____

_____

_____

The Freedom of Forgiveness

Galatians 5:1
It is for freedom that Christ has set us free.

Psalm 119:45
I will walk about in freedom,

for I have sought out your precepts., O LORD.

Acts 2:38
Repent and be baptized, every one of you, in the name of Jesus Christ for the forgiveness of your sins. And you will receive the gift of the Holy Spirit.

Acts 10:43
All the prophets testify about Jesus that everyone who believes in him receives forgiveness of sins through his name.

2 Corinthians 3:17
The Lord is the Spirit, and where the Spirit of the
Lord is, there is freedom.

Galatians 5:13
You ... were called to be free.

Ephesians 1:3–7
Praise be to the God and Father of our Lord Jesus
Christ, who has blessed us in the heavenly realms
with every spiritual blessing in Christ. For he chose
us in him before the creation of the world to be
holy and blameless in his sight. In love he predestined us to be adopted as his sons through Jesus
Christ, in accordance with his pleasure and will—to
the praise of his glorious grace, which he has freely
given us in the One he loves. In Christ we have
redemption through his blood, the forgiveness of
sins, in accordance with the riches of God's grace.

Ephesians 3:12
In Christ and through faith in him we may
approach God with freedom and confidence.

James 1:25
The man who looks intently into the perfect law
that gives freedom, and continues to do this, not
forgetting what he has heard, but doing it—he will
be blessed in what he does.

Hebrews 9:15
Christ is the mediator of a new covenant, that
those who are called may receive the promised
eternal inheritance—now that he has died as a
ransom to set them free from the sins committed
under the first covenant.

Romans 8:21
Creation itself will be liberated from its bondage
to decay and brought into the glorious freedom of
the children of God.

Colossians 1:22–23
God has reconciled you by Christ's physical body
through death to present you holy in his sight,
without blemish and free from accusation—if you
continue in your faith, established and firm, not
moved from the hope held out in the gospel.

John 8:36
If the Son sets you free, you will be free indeed.

Romans 8:1–2
There is now no condemnation for those who are
in Christ Jesus, because through Christ Jesus the
law of the Spirit of life set me free from the law of
sin and death.

My favorite verses about the Freedom of Forgiveness

_____

_____

_____

_____

_____

_____

_____

_____

_____

_____

_____

_____

_____

_____

_____

Thoughts and Reflections about the Freedom of Forgiveness

_____

_____

_____

_____

_____

_____

_____

_____

_____

_____

_____

_____

_____

_____

_____

Certainty in God

Hebrews 11:1
Faith is being sure of what we hope for and certain of what we do not see.

Romans 8:38–39
Neither death nor life, neither angels nor demons, neither the present nor the future, nor any powers, neither height nor depth, nor anything else in all creation, will be able to separate us from the love of God that is in Christ Jesus our Lord.

Isaiah 54:10
"Though the mountains be shaken
    and the hills be removed,
yet my unfailing love for you will not be shaken
    or my covenant of peace be removed,"
    says the LORD, who has compassion on you.

John 10:27-29
Jesus said, "My sheep listen to my voice; I know
them, and they follow me. I give them eternal life,
and they shall never perish; no one can snatch
them out of my hand. My Father, who has given
them to me, is greater than all; no one can snatch
them out of my Father's hand."

2 Timothy 1:12
I know whom I have believed, and am convinced
that he is able to guard what I have entrusted to
him for that day.

1 Timothy 3:13
Those who have served well gain an excellent
standing and great assurance in their faith in
Christ Jesus.

Hebrews 10:19, 22
Since we have confidence to enter the Most Holy
Place by the blood of Jesus ... let us draw near to
God with a sincere heart in full assurance of faith,
having our hearts sprinkled to cleanse us from a
guilty conscience and having our bodies washed
with pure water.

1 John 5:14–15

This is the confidence we have in approaching God: that if we ask anything according to his will, he hears us. And if we know that he hears us— whatever we ask—we know that we have what we asked of him.

Proverbs 3:26

The LORD will be your confidence

and will keep your foot from being snared.

Hebrews 13:6

We say with confidence,

"The LORD is my helper; I will not be afraid.

What can man do to me?"

Psalm 27:3, 5

Though an army besiege me,

my heart will not fear;

though war break out against me,

even then will I be confident. ...

For in the day of trouble

God will keep me safe in his dwelling.

Psalm 23:4

Even though I walk

> through the valley of the shadow of death,

I will fear no evil,

> for you are with me, O LORD;

your rod and your staff,

> they comfort me.

1 John 4:16–17

We know and rely on the love God has for us. God is love. Whoever lives in love lives in God, and God in him. In this way, love is made complete among us so that we will have confidence on the day of judgment, because in this world we are like him.

Isaiah 32:17

The fruit of righteousness will be peace;

> the effect of righteousness will be quietness

and confidence forever.

1 John 2:28
Continue in Christ, so that when he appears we may be confident and unashamed before him at his coming.

Hebrews 4:16
Let us then approach the throne of grace with confidence, so that we may receive mercy and find grace to help us in our time of need.

1 John 3:21–24
Dear friends, if our hearts do not condemn us, we have confidence before God and receive from him anything we ask, because we obey his commands and do what pleases him. And this is his command: to believe in the name of his Son, Jesus Christ, and to love one another as he commanded us. Those who obey his commands live in him, and he in them. And this is how we know that he lives in us: We know it by the Spirit he gave us.

Hebrews 10:35–37

Do not throw away your confidence; it will be richly rewarded. You need to persevere so that when you have done the will of God, you will receive what he has promised. For in just a very little while,

"He who is coming will come and will not delay."

Jeremiah 17:7–8

Blessed is the man who trusts in the LORD,

>   whose confidence is in him.

He will be like a tree planted by the water

>   that sends out its roots by the stream.

It does not fear when heat comes;

>   its leaves are always green.

It has no worries in a year of drought

>   and never fails to bear fruit."

My favorite verses about Certainty in God

_____

_____

_____

_____

_____

_____

_____

_____

_____

_____

_____

_____

_____

_____

_____

_____

_____

_____

_____

_____

Thoughts and Reflections about Certainty in God

_____

_____

_____

_____

_____

_____

_____

_____

_____

_____

_____

_____

_____

_____

_____

_____

Strength to Resist Temptation

1 Corinthians 10:13
No temptation has seized you except what is common to man. And God is faithful; he will not let you be tempted beyond what you can bear. But when you are tempted, he will also provide a way out so that you can stand up under it.

James 1:12
Blessed is the man who perseveres under trial, because when he has stood the test, he will receive the crown of life that God has promised to those who love him.

James 4:7
Submit yourselves ... to God. Resist the devil, and he will flee from you.

Hebrews 2:18
Because Jesus himself suffered when he was tempted, he is able to help those who are being tempted.

Hebrews 4:14–16

Since we have a great high priest who has gone through the heavens, Jesus the Son of God, let us hold firmly to the faith we profess. For we do not have a high priest who is unable to sympathize with our weaknesses, but we have one who has been tempted in every way, just as we are—yet was without sin. Let us then approach the throne of grace with confidence, so that we may receive mercy and find grace to help us in our time of need.

Galatians 5:1

It is for freedom that Christ has set us free. Stand firm, then, and do not let yourselves be burdened again by a yoke of slavery.

Ephesians 6:10–11

Be strong in the Lord and in his mighty power. Put on the full armor of God so that you can take your stand against the devil's schemes.

Psalm 119:11
I have hidden your word in my heart, O LORD,

that I might not sin against you.

Romans 6:14
Sin shall not be your master, because you are not
under law, but under grace.

2 Corinthians 12:9
The Lord said to me, "My grace is sufficient for
you, for my power is made perfect in weakness."
Therefore I will boast all the more gladly about my
weaknesses, so that Christ's power may rest on me.

1 Peter 1:7
Trials have come so that your faith—of greater
worth than gold, which perishes even though
refined by fire—may be proved genuine and may
result in praise, glory and honor when Jesus Christ
is revealed.

Psalm 46:1–3

God is our refuge and strength,

> an ever-present help in trouble.

Therefore we will not fear, though the earth give way

> and the mountains fall into the heart of the sea,

though its waters roar and foam

> and the mountains quake with their surging.

Psalm 68:19

Praise be to the LORD, to God our Savior,

> who daily bears our burdens.

Proverbs 28:13

He who conceals his sins does not prosper,

> but whoever confesses and renounces them

finds mercy.

Isaiah 59:1

Surely the arm of the LORD is not too short to save,

> nor his ear too dull to hear.

1 John 1:9
If we confess our sins, God is faithful and just and will forgive us our sins and purify us from all unrighteousness.

1 John 4:4
The one who is in you is greater than the one who is in the world.

Joshua 1:9
Be strong and courageous. Do not be terrified; do not be discouraged, for the LORD your God will be with you wherever you go.

Jude 1:24–25
To him who is able to keep you from falling and to present you before his glorious presence without fault and with great joy—to the only God our Savior be glory, majesty, power and authority, through Jesus Christ our Lord, before all ages, now and forevermore! Amen.

2 Peter 2:9
The Lord knows how to rescue godly men from trials.

2 Timothy 4:17
The Lord stood at my side and gave me strength.

Philippians 4:13
I can do everything through Christ who gives me strength.

Habakkuk 3:19
The Sovereign LORD is my strength;

    he makes my feet like the feet of a deer,

    he enables me to go on the heights.

My favorite verses about Strength to Resist Temptation

_____
_____
_____
_____
_____
_____
_____
_____
_____
_____
_____
_____
_____
_____
_____
_____
_____

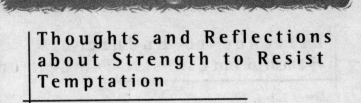

Thoughts and Reflections about Strength to Resist Temptation

_____

_____

_____

_____

_____

_____

_____

_____

_____

_____

_____

_____

_____

_____

_____

_____

_____

_____

Patience to Endure Hard Times

James 1:2–4, 12

Consider it pure joy, my brothers, whenever you face trials of many kinds, because you know that the testing of your faith develops perseverance. Perseverance must finish its work so that you may be mature and complete, not lacking anything. . . .

Blessed is the man who perseveres under trial, because when he has stood the test, he will receive the crown of life that God has promised to those who love him.

Romans 8:38–39

Neither death nor life, neither angels nor demons, neither the present nor the future, nor any powers, neither height nor depth, nor anything else in all creation, will be able to separate us from the love of God that is in Christ Jesus our Lord.

Romans 5:3–4

We also rejoice in our sufferings, because we know that suffering produces perseverance; persever-ance, character; and character, hope.

2 Corinthians 4:8–10, 16–18

We are hard pressed on every side, but not crushed; perplexed, but not in despair; persecuted, but not abandoned; struck down, but not destroyed. We always carry around in our body the death of Jesus, so that the life of Jesus may also be revealed in our body. ... Therefore we do not lose heart. Though outwardly we are wasting away, yet inwardly we are being renewed day by day. For our light and momentary troubles are achieving for us an eternal glory that far outweighs them all. So we fix our eyes not on what is seen, but on what is unseen. For what is seen is temporary, but what is unseen is eternal.

Psalm 121:1–2

I lift up my eyes to the hills—

   where does my help come from?

My help comes from the LORD,

   the Maker of heaven and earth.

Psalm 147:3

The LORD heals the brokenhearted

   and binds up their wounds.

Isaiah 41:10

"Do not fear, for I am with you;

   do not be dismayed, for I am your God.

I will strengthen you and help you;

   I will uphold you with my righteous right
hand."

Romans 8:28

In all things God works for the good of those who
love him, who have been called according to his
purpose.

Isaiah 43:2

"When you pass through the waters,

   I will be with you;

and when you pass through the rivers,

   they will not sweep over you.

When you walk through the fire,

   you will not be burned;

   the flames will not set you ablaze,"

      says the LORD.

Philippians 4:6–7

Do not be anxious about anything, but in every-thing, by prayer and petition, with thanksgiving, present your requests to God. And the peace of God, which transcends all understanding, will guard your hearts and your minds in Christ Jesus.

Philippians 4:13

I can do everything through God who gives me strength.

Exodus 14:14
The LORD will fight for you; you need only to be still.

Psalm 31:7
I will be glad and rejoice in your love, O LORD,

> for you saw my affliction

> and knew the anguish of my soul.

Psalm 138:7
Though I walk in the midst of trouble,

> you preserve my life, O LORD;

you stretch out your hand

> against the anger of my foes,

> with your right hand you save me.

Isaiah 40:31
Those who hope in the LORD

> will renew their strength.

They will soar on wings like eagles;

> they will run and not grow weary,

> they will walk and not be faint.

Lamentations 3:24–26

I say to myself, "The Lord is my portion;

therefore I will wait for him."

The Lord is good to those whose hope is in him,

to the one who seeks him;

it is good to wait quietly

for the salvation of the Lord.

Nahum 1:7

The Lord is good,

a refuge in times of trouble.

He cares for those who trust in him.

Matthew 6:34

Do not worry about tomorrow, for tomorrow will worry about itself.

John 14:1

Jesus said, "Do not let your hearts be troubled. Trust in God; trust also in me."

2 Corinthians 1:3–4

Praise be to the God and Father of our Lord Jesus
Christ, the Father of compassion and the God of
all comfort, who comforts us in all our troubles, so
that we can comfort those in any trouble with the
comfort we ourselves have received from God.

Hebrews 12:10–11

Our fathers disciplined us for a little while as they
thought best; but God disciplines us for our good,
that we may share in his holiness. No discipline
seems pleasant at the time, but painful. Later on,
however, it produces a harvest of righteousness
and peace for those who have been trained by it.

Hebrews 13:5

God has said, "Never will I leave you;

never will I forsake you."

1 Peter 5:7
Cast all your anxiety on God because he cares for you.

1 Peter 5:10
The God of all grace, who called you to his eternal glory in Christ, after you have suffered a little while, will himself restore you and make you strong, firm and steadfast. To him be the power for ever and ever. Amen.

My favorite verses about Patience to Endure Hard Times

_____

_____

_____

_____

_____

_____

_____

_____

_____

_____

_____

_____

_____

_____

_____

Thoughts and Reflections about Patience to Endure Hard Times

_____

_____

_____

_____

_____

_____

_____

_____

_____

_____

_____

_____

_____

_____

_____

_____

_____

_____

Chapter Six

How Does God Value Your Relationships?

Promises for Your Friends and Family

Thank you, God, that you designed me to live in community with others and that you have brought people into my life to challenge, influence, and love me. Thank you that you value my relationships and care about every detail and person in my life. You are a wonderful God.

Your Family

Ephesians 6:1–3
Children, obey your parents in the Lord, for this is right. "Honor your father and mother"—which is the first commandment with a promise—"that it may go well with you and that you may enjoy long life on the earth."

Psalm 68:5
A father to the fatherless ... is God in his holy dwelling.

Psalm 103:13
As a father has compassion on his children,

> so the LORD has compassion

> on those who fear him.

Psalm 22:10
From birth I was cast upon you;

> from my mother's womb

> you have been my God.

motivation achievement diligence

Psalm 139:13
You created my inmost being, O LORD;

> you knit me together in my mother's womb.

Psalm 127:1
Unless the LORD builds the house,

> its builders labor in vain.

Psalm 103:17
From everlasting to everlasting

> the LORD's love is with those who fear him,
>
> and his righteousness
>
> with their children's children.

Proverbs 17:6
Children's children are a crown to the aged,

> and parents are the pride of their children.

Proverbs 6:20–23
Keep your father's commands

and do not forsake your mother's teaching.

Bind them upon your heart forever;

fasten them around your neck.

When you walk, they will guide you;

when you sleep, they will watch over you;

when you awake, they will speak to you.

For these commands are a lamp,

this teaching is a light,

and the corrections of discipline

are the way to life.

Psalm 68:6
God sets the lonely in families.

Mark 3:35
Jesus said, "Whoever does God's will is my brother
and sister and mother."

motivation   achievement
diligence

Isaiah 32:18

My people will live in peaceful dwelling places,

in secure homes,

in undisturbed places of rest.

Proverbs 3:33

The LORD blesses the home of the righteous.

My favorite verses about family

_____

_____

_____

_____

_____

_____

_____

_____

_____

_____

_____

_____

_____

_____

_____

_____

_____

_____

Thoughts and Reflections about family

_____

_____

_____

_____

_____

_____

_____

_____

_____

_____

_____

_____

_____

_____

_____

Your Marriage

Genesis 2:18
The LORD God said, "It is not good for the man to be alone. I will make a helper suitable for him."

Matthew 19:4-6
At the beginning the Creator "made them male and female," and said, "For this reason a man will leave his father and mother and be united to his wife, and the two will become one flesh." So they are no longer two, but one.

Proverbs 5:18-19
May your fountain be blessed,

and may you rejoice in the wife of your youth. ...

May you ever be captivated by her love.

Proverbs 18:22
He who finds a wife finds what is good

and receives favor from the LORD.

Proverbs 31:10–11, 28–30

A wife of noble character who can find?

She is worth far more than rubies.

Her husband has full confidence in her

and lacks nothing of value. . . .

Her children arise and call her blessed;

her husband also, and he praises her:

"Many women do noble things,

but you surpass them all."

Charm is deceptive, and beauty is fleeting;

but a woman who fears the LORD

is to be praised.

Ecclesiastes 4:9–10

Two are better than one,

because they have a good return

for their work:

If one falls down,

his friend can help him up.

Song of Songs 8:7
Many waters cannot quench love;

> rivers cannot wash it away.

If one were to give

> all the wealth of his house for love,

> it would be utterly scorned.

Proverbs 19:14
Houses and wealth are inherited from parents,

> but a prudent wife is from the LORD.

Proverbs 12:4
A wife of noble character is her husband's crown.

Song of Songs 7:10
I belong to my lover,

> and his desire is for me.

James 5:16
Confess your sins to each other and pray for each other so that you may be healed. The prayer of a righteous man is powerful and effective.

1 Corinthians 13:4–8
Love is patient, love is kind. It does not envy, it
does not boast, it is not proud. It is not rude, it is
not self-seeking, it is not easily angered, it keeps
no record of wrongs. Love does not delight in evil
but rejoices with the truth. It always protects,
always trusts, always hopes, always perseveres.
Love never fails.

My favorite verses about marriage

_____
_____
_____
_____
_____
_____
_____
_____
_____
_____
_____
_____
_____
_____
_____
_____
_____
_____

Thoughts and Reflections about marriage

_____

_____

_____

_____

_____

_____

_____

_____

_____

_____

_____

_____

_____

_____

Your Friends

Proverbs 18:24
A man of many companions may come to ruin,

but there is a friend

who sticks closer than a brother.

Proverbs 27:17
As iron sharpens iron,

so one man sharpens another.

Ecclesiastes 4:9–10
Two are better than one,

because they have a good return

for their work:

If one falls down,

his friend can help him up.

Galatians 6:2
Carry each other's burdens, and in this way you
will fulfill the law of Christ.

Proverbs 13:20
He who walks with the wise grows wise.

Proverbs 17:17
A friend loves at all times,

and a brother is born for adversity.

Proverbs 27:6
Wounds from a friend can be trusted.

Matthew 18:20
Jesus said, "For where two or three come together
in my name, there am I with them."

John 15:13
Greater love has no one than this, that he lay
down his life for his friends.

John 15:15

Jesus said, "I no longer call you servants, because a servant does not know his master's business. Instead, I have called you friends, for everything that I learned from my Father I have made known to you."

Job 16:20–21

My intercessor is my friend

    as my eyes pour out tears to God;

on behalf of a man he pleads with God

    as a man pleads for his friend.

Proverbs 17:9

He who covers over an offense promotes love,

    but whoever repeats the matter

    separates close friends.

Proverbs 27:9

Perfume and incense bring joy to the heart,

    and the pleasantness of one's friend

    springs from his earnest counsel.

Ecclesiastes 4:12

Though one may be overpowered,

two can defend themselves.

A cord of three strands is not quickly broken.

1 Samuel 20:42

Jonathan said to David, "Go in peace, for we have sworn friendship with each other in the name of the LORD, saying, 'The LORD is witness between you and me, and between your descendants and my descendants forever.'"

My favorite verses about friendship

_____

_____

_____

_____

_____

_____

_____

_____

_____

_____

_____

_____

_____

_____

_____

_____

Thoughts and Reflections about friendship

_____

_____

_____

_____

_____

_____

_____

_____

_____

_____

_____

_____

_____

_____

Your Church

1 Corinthians 12:27
You are the body of Christ, and each one of you is a part of it.

Ephesians 4:4–6
There is one body and one Spirit—just as you were called to one hope when you were called—one Lord, one faith, one baptism; one God and Father of all, who is over all and through all and in all.

Romans 12:4–8
Just as each of us has one body with many members, and these members do not all have the same function, so in Christ we who are many form one body, and each member belongs to all the others. We have different gifts, according to the grace given us. If a man's gift is prophesying, let him use it in proportion to his faith. If it is serving, let him serve; if it is teaching, let him teach; if it is encouraging, let him encourage; if it is contributing to the needs of others, let him give generously; if it is leadership, let him govern diligently; if it is showing mercy, let him do it cheerfully.

Ephesians 4:11–13

It was Christ who gave some to be apostles, some to be prophets, some to be evangelists, and some to be pastors and teachers, to prepare God's people for works of service, so that the body of Christ may be built up until we all reach unity in the faith and in the knowledge of the Son of God and become mature, attaining to the whole measure of the fullness of Christ.

1 Corinthians 12:12–13

The body is a unit, though it is made up of many parts; and though all its parts are many, they form one body. So it is with Christ. For we were all baptized by one Spirit into one body—whether Jews or Greeks, slave or free—and we were all given the one Spirit to drink.

Ephesians 2:21–22

In Christ the whole building is joined together and rises to become a holy temple in the Lord. And in him you too are being built together to become a dwelling in which God lives by his Spirit.

James 5:16
Confess your sins to each other and pray for each other so that you may be healed. The prayer of a righteous man is powerful and effective.

Psalm 133:1
How good and pleasant it is
    when brothers live together in unity!

1 Corinthians 12:28–31
In the church God has appointed first of all apostles, second prophets, third teachers, then workers of miracles, also those having gifts of healing, those able to help others, those with gifts of administration, and those speaking in different kinds of tongues. Are all apostles? Are all prophets? Are all teachers? Do all work miracles? Do all have gifts of healing? Do all speak in tongues? Do all interpret? But eagerly desire the greater gifts.

Ephesians 3:10–12

God's intent was that now, through the church, the manifold wisdom of God should be made known to the rulers and authorities in the heavenly realms, according to his eternal purpose which he accomplished in Christ Jesus our Lord. In him and through faith in him we may approach God with freedom and confidence.

My favorite verses about church

_____

_____

_____

_____

_____

_____

_____

_____

_____

_____

_____

_____

_____

_____

_____

_____

_____

_____

Thoughts and Reflections about church

_____

_____

_____

_____

_____

_____

_____

_____

_____

_____

_____

_____

_____

_____

_____

_____

Chapter Seven

How Should You Live Now?

Promises for the Christian Walk

Thank you, my loving Father, that you are not finished with me yet. As you and I journey through this life together, please make me more into your likeness so that you will be satisfied with the person I am becoming in you.

Your Finances

Malachi 3:10

"Bring the whole tithe into the storehouse, that there may be food in my house. Test me in this," says the LORD Almighty, "and see if I will not throw open the floodgates of heaven and pour out so much blessing that you will not have room enough for it."

2 Corinthians 9:7

Each man should give what he has decided in his heart to give, not reluctantly or under compulsion, for God loves a cheerful giver.

Proverbs 3:9–10

Honor the LORD with your wealth,

with the firstfruits of all your crops;

then your barns will be filled to overflowing,

and your vats will brim over with new wine.

Philippians 4:11–12
I have learned to be content whatever the circumstances. I know what it is to be in need, and I know what it is to have plenty. I have learned the secret of being content in any and every situation, whether well fed or hungry, whether living in plenty or in want.

Philippians 4:19
God will meet all your needs according to his glorious riches in Christ Jesus.

1 Timothy 6:6
Godliness with contentment is great gain.

Proverbs 11:28
Whoever trusts in his riches will fall,
but the righteous will thrive like a green leaf.

Proverbs 19:1
Better a poor man whose walk is blameless
than a fool whose lips are perverse.

Proverbs 21:20
In the house of the wise are stores of choice food and oil.

Matthew 6:31–33
Do not worry, saying, "What shall we eat?" or "What shall we drink?" or "What shall we wear?" For the pagans run after all these things, and your heavenly Father knows that you need them. But seek first his kingdom and his righteousness, and all these things will be given to you as well.

Luke 6:38
Give, and it will be given to you. A good measure, pressed down, shaken together and running over, will be poured in your lap. For with the measure you use, it will be measured to you.

Romans 13:8
Let no debt remain outstanding, except the continuing debt to love one another, for he who loves his fellowman has fulfilled the law.

Hebrews 13:5
Keep your lives free from the love of money and
be content with what you have, because God has
said,

"Never will I leave you;

never will I forsake you."

Proverbs 13:11
He who gathers money little

by little makes it grow

Ecclesiasties 7:12
Wisdom is a shelter

as a money is a shelter,

but the advantage of knowledge is this:

that wisdom preserves the life of its possessor.

My favorite verses about finances

Thoughts and Reflections about finances

_____

_____

_____

_____

_____

_____

_____

_____

_____

_____

_____

_____

_____

_____

_____

_____

Your Work

Colossians 3:23–24
Whatever you do, work at it with all your heart, as working for the Lord, not for men, since you know that you will receive an inheritance from the Lord as a reward.

Luke 16:10
Whoever can be trusted with very little can also be trusted with much.

Proverbs 10:4
Diligent hands bring wealth.

1 Corinthians 15:58
Always give yourselves fully to the work of the Lord, because you know that your labor in the Lord is not in vain.

Philippians 1:6
God who began a good work in you will carry it on to completion until the day of Christ Jesus.

Hebrews 4:9–10
There remains ... a Sabbath-rest for the people of God; for anyone who enters God's rest also rests from his own work, just as God did from his.

Hebrews 13:20–21
May the God of peace, who through the blood of the eternal covenant brought back from the dead our Lord Jesus, that great Shepherd of the sheep, equip you with everything good for doing his will, and may he work in us what is pleasing to him, through Jesus Christ, to whom be glory for ever and ever.

Proverbs 11:3
The integrity of the upright guides them.

Hebrews 6:10
God is not unjust; he will not forget your work and the love you have shown him as you have helped his people.

Philippians 2:13
It is God who works in you to will and to act according to his good purpose.

2 Corinthians 9:8
God is able to make all grace abound to you, so that in all things at all times, having all that you need, you will abound in every good work.

1 Corinthians 3:11–14
No one can lay any foundation other than the one already laid, which is Jesus Christ. If any man builds on this foundation using gold, silver, costly stones, wood, hay or straw, his work will be shown for what it is, because the Day will bring it to light. It will be revealed with fire, and the fire will test the quality of each man's work. If what he has built survives, he will receive his reward.

1 Corinthians 3:9

We are God's fellow workers; you are God's field,
God's building.

Psalm 41:12

In my integrity you uphold me, O LORD,

and set me in your presence forever.

Ecclesiastes 5:12

The sleep of a laborer is sweet.

My favorite verses about work

_____

_____

_____

_____

_____

_____

_____

_____

_____

_____

_____

_____

_____

_____

_____

_____

_____

_____

_____

Thoughts and Reflections about work

_____

_____

_____

_____

_____

_____

_____

_____

_____

_____

_____

_____

_____

_____

_____

_____

_____

_____

Clay in the Potter's Hands

Isaiah 64:8

O LORD, you are our Father.

We are the clay, you are the potter;

we are all the work of your hand.

Jeremiah 18:6

"Can I not do with you as this potter does?" declares the LORD. "Like clay in the hand of the potter, so are you in my hand."

2 Corinthians 4:6–7

God made his light shine in our hearts to give us the light of the knowledge of the glory of God in the face of Christ. But we have this treasure in jars of clay to show that this all-surpassing power is from God and not from us.

Philippians 1:6

God who began a good work in you will carry it on to completion until the day of Christ Jesus.

Philippians 2:12–13

As you have always obeyed—not only in my presence, but now much more in my absence—continue to work out your salvation with fear and trembling, for it is God who works in you to will and to act according to his good purpose.

Psalm 12:6

The words of the LORD are flawless,

> like silver refined in a furnace of clay,
>
> purified seven times.

Psalm 138:8

The LORD will fulfill his purpose for me;

> your love, O LORD, endures forever—
>
> do not abandon the works of your hands.

1 Samuel 16:7

The LORD does not look at the things man looks at. Man looks at the outward appearance, but the LORD looks at the heart.

Genesis 1:27–28

God created man in his own image,

in the image of God he created him;

male and female he created them.

God blessed them. ...

Psalm 139:13–17

You created my inmost being, O LORD;

    you knit me together in my mother's womb.

I praise you because I am

    fearfully and wonderfully made;

    your works are wonderful,

    I know that full well.

My frame was not hidden from you

    when I was made in the secret place.

When I was woven together

    in the depths of the earth,

    your eyes saw my unformed body.

All the days ordained for me

    were written in your book

    before one of them came to be.

How precious to me are your thoughts, O God!

    How vast is the sum of them!

2 Timothy 1:12

I am not ashamed, because I know whom I have
believed, and am convinced that God is able to
guard what I have entrusted to him for that day.

Psalm 100:3

Know that the LORD is God.

> It is he who made us, and we are his;

> we are his people, the sheep of his pasture.

Ecclesiastes 3:11

God has made everything beautiful in its time.

My favorite verses about being Clay in the Potter's hands

_____

_____

_____

_____

_____

_____

_____

_____

_____

_____

_____

_____

_____

_____

_____

_____

Thoughts and Reflections about being Clay in the Potter's hands

_____

_____

_____

_____

_____

_____

_____

_____

_____

_____

_____

_____

_____

_____

Running the Race

Hebrews 12:1

Since we are surrounded by such a great cloud of witnesses, let us throw off everything that hinders and the sin that so easily entangles, and let us run with perseverance the race marked out for us.

Romans 5:3–4

We also rejoice in our sufferings, because we know that suffering produces perseverance; perseverance, character; and character, hope.

1 Corinthians 9:27

I beat my body and make it my slave so that after I have preached to others, I myself will not be disqualified for the prize.

Revelation 2:19
Jesus said, "I know your deeds, your love and faith, your service and perseverance, and that you are now doing more than you did at first."

Matthew 24:13
He who stands firm to the end will be saved.

Ephesians 6:10–13
Be strong in the Lord and in his mighty power. Put on the full armor of God so that you can take your stand against the devil's schemes. For our struggle is not against flesh and blood, but against the rulers, against the authorities, against the powers of this dark world and against the spiritual forces of evil in the heavenly realms. Therefore put on the full armor of God, so that when the day of evil comes, you may be able to stand your ground, and after you have done everything, to stand.

2 Thessalonians 3:5
May the Lord direct your hearts into God's love
and Christ's perseverance.

Isaiah 30:19–21
O people of Zion, who live in Jerusalem, you will
weep no more. How gracious the LORD will be
when you cry for help! As soon as he hears, he will
answer you. Although the LORD gives you the bread
of adversity and the water of affliction, your
teachers will be hidden no more; with your own
eyes you will see them. Whether you turn to the
right or to the left, your ears will hear a voice
behind you, saying, "This is the way; walk in it."

Matthew 6:19–21
Do not store up for yourselves treasures on earth,
where moth and rust destroy, and where thieves
break in and steal. But store up for yourselves
treasures in heaven, where moth and rust do not
destroy, and where thieves do not break in and
steal. For where your treasure is, there your heart
will be also.

Matthew 17:20
If you have faith as small as a mustard seed, you
can say to this mountain, "Move from here to
there" and it will move. Nothing will be impossible
for you.

James 1:3–4
The testing of your faith develops perseverance.
Perseverance must finish its work so that you may
be mature and complete, not lacking anything.

My favorite verses about Running the Race

_____
_____
_____
_____
_____
_____
_____
_____
_____
_____
_____
_____
_____
_____
_____
_____
_____
_____
_____

Thoughts and Reflections about Running the Race

_____

_____

_____

_____

_____

_____

_____

_____

_____

_____

_____

_____

_____

_____

_____

Growing in God

Ephesians 4:15
Speaking the truth in love, we will in all things
grow up into him who is the Head, that is, Christ.

Matthew 5:13–14
You are the salt of the earth. ... You are the light
of the world. A city on a hill cannot be hidden.

2 Corinthians 4:6
God, who said, "Let light shine out of darkness,"
made his light shine in our hearts to give us the
light of the knowledge of the glory of God in the
face of Christ.

Ephesians 6:11
Put on the full armor of God so that you can take
your stand against the devil's schemes.

2 Corinthians 4:16–18

We do not lose heart. Though outwardly we are wasting away, yet inwardly we are being renewed day by day. For our light and momentary troubles are achieving for us an eternal glory that far outweighs them all. So we fix our eyes not on what is seen, but on what is unseen. For what is seen is temporary, but what is unseen is eternal.

Ephesians 6:14–18

Stand firm then, with the belt of truth buckled around your waist, with the breastplate of righteousness in place, and with your feet fitted with the readiness that comes from the gospel of peace. In addition to all this, take up the shield of faith, with which you can extinguish all the flaming arrows of the evil one. Take the helmet of salvation and the sword of the Spirit, which is the word of God. And pray in the Spirit on all occasions with all kinds of prayers and requests. With this in mind, be alert and always keep on praying for all the saints.

1 John 4:4

The one who is in you is greater than the one who is in the world.

Galatians 5:22–25

The fruit of the Spirit is love, joy, peace, patience, kindness, goodness, faithfulness, gentleness and self-control. Against such things there is no law. Those who belong to Christ Jesus have crucified the sinful nature with its passions and desires. Since we live by the Spirit, let us keep in step with the Spirit.

Proverbs 21:21

He who pursues righteousness and love

finds life, prosperity and honor.

Matthew 5:6

Blessed are those who hunger

and thirst for righteousness,

for they will be filled.

John 1:12–13

To all who received Christ, to those who believed in his name, he gave the right to become children of God—children born not of natural descent, nor of human decision or a husband's will, but born of God.

Matthew 7:24–25

Jesus said, "Everyone who hears these words of mine and puts them into practice is like a wise man who built his house on the rock. The rain came down, the streams rose, and the winds blew and beat against that house; yet it did not fall, because it had its foundation on the rock."

My favorite verses about Growing in God

_____

_____

_____

_____

_____

_____

_____

_____

_____

_____

_____

_____

_____

_____

_____

_____

_____

_____

_____

_____

Thoughts and Reflections about Growing in God

_____

_____

_____

_____

_____

_____

_____

_____

_____

_____

_____

_____

_____

_____

_____

_____

_____

Heaven: Your Ultimate Reward

Matthew 5:11–12

Jesus said, "Blessed are you when people insult you, persecute you and falsely say all kinds of evil against you because of me. Rejoice and be glad, because great is your reward in heaven.

Matthew 6:20–21

Store up for yourselves treasures in heaven, where moth and rust do not destroy, and where thieves do not break in and steal. For where your treasure is, there your heart will be also.

Matthew 10:32

Jesus said, "Whoever acknowledges me before men, I will also acknowledge him before my Father in heaven."

Philippians 3:20–21
Our citizenship is in heaven. And we eagerly await
a Savior from there, the Lord Jesus Christ, who, by
the power that enables him to bring everything
under his control, will transform our lowly bodies
so that they will be like his glorious body.

1 Peter 1:3–5
Praise be to the God and Father of our Lord Jesus
Christ! In his great mercy he has given us new
birth into a living hope through the resurrection of
Jesus Christ from the dead, and into an inheritance
that can never perish, spoil or fade—kept in
heaven for you, who through faith are shielded by
God's power until the coming of the salvation that
is ready to be revealed in the last time.

2 Peter 3:13
In keeping with God's promise we are looking for-
ward to a new heaven and a new earth, the home
of righteousness.

1 Thessalonians 4:16–17

The Lord himself will come down from heaven,
with a loud command, with the voice of the
archangel and with the trumpet call of God, and
the dead in Christ will rise first. After that, we who
are still alive and are left will be caught up
together with them in the clouds to meet the Lord
in the air. And so we will be with the Lord forever.

Revelation 21:1–5

I saw a new heaven and a new earth, for the first
heaven and the first earth had passed away, and
there was no longer any sea. I saw the Holy City, the
new Jerusalem, coming down out of heaven from
God, prepared as a bride beautifully dressed for her
husband. And I heard a loud voice from the throne
saying, "Now the dwelling of God is with men, and
he will live with them. They will be his people, and
God himself will be with them and be their God. He
will wipe every tear from their eyes. There will be no
more death or mourning or crying or pain, for the old
order of things has passed away." He who was seated
on the throne said, "I am making everything new!"

My favorite verses about heaven

_____

_____

_____

_____

_____

_____

_____

_____

_____

_____

_____

_____

_____

_____

_____

_____

Thoughts and Reflections about heaven

_____

_____

_____

_____

_____

_____

_____

_____

_____

_____

_____

_____

_____

_____

_____

_____

_____

_____